fest
The Transformation of Everyday

by
Gerhard Marcel Martin

Translated and with an Introduction by
M. Douglas Meeks

Fortress Press   Philadelphia

This book is a translation of *Fest und Alltag. Bausteine zu einer Theorie des Festes,* copyrighted © 1973 by Verlag W. Kohlham-mer GmbH in Stuttgart, Germany.

Biblical quotations from the Revised Standard Version of the Bible, copyrighted 1946, 1952, © 1971, 1973 by the Division of Christian Education of the National Council of the Churches of Christ in the U.S.A., are used by permission.

Library of Congress Catalog Card Number 76-007865

ISBN 0-8006-1233-7

5310E76   Printed in U.S.A.   1-1233

CONTENTS

To Jörg Panzer

and all those who live with

protest and joy

The smallest analysis will discover that there are two different sorts of liberation, which can be distinguished very easily, since they are contrasted in a structural way:

a. freedom which is integrated in the everyday situation . . .

b. the expectation of going on a trip, the demand for a break in experience, the wish to escape through worldliness, holidays, LSD, nature, debauchery, and mental disease.

Henri Lefebvre
Everyday Life in the Modern World
(translation altered)

PREFACE

What is the essence of fest? What is its function? How can it be used and misused? These are the most general questions behind all sorts of festive activities and experiences. They are theoretical questions, somehow academic in comparison with reports about real fests and concrete advice about how to celebrate. Nevertheless the following contributions to theory are not meant to be only theoretical discussions within philosophical and theological frameworks—although this also seems to be a need. They are based on material from history and my own experience and tend toward a new praxis. The critical theory of past and present fests should deal with realities and possibilities of celebrations and festivities. For the essence will reveal itself only in concrete phenomena; the general can be seen only in particular details. That is why theory about and for praxis can be narrative, should deal with examples, and tries to remain close to reality to avoid false abstraction.

Thus the history of fest and historical experience in general may not simply be excluded. What is wrong and right with our present praxis may become clear precisely by means of confronting it with different descriptions and practices from former times. The material which should be taken into consideration is almost unlimited. Strictly speaking, the entire history of religions and civilizations would have to pass in review. We would be caught up by an endless sequence of images: from rituals to mystical ecstasy, from Dionysian festivals to military parades, from worship in ancient synagogues to coronations of emperors, and from court balls to the marriage of Mack the Knife. The only way to avoid an unmanageable inflation of images and material is a concrete and conscious self-limitation.

v

Indeed, three limitations of this book need to be mentioned specifically.

As far as a first limitation is concerned, I hope that my essay is a contribution to the present discussions of theory and praxis of fest. This debate is in part determined by possibilities and abilities to celebrate that are currently available to us as persons and communities in society. One of the leading questions of the last ten years has been that of how to reconcile and integrate the different spheres of aesthetics and ethics, of moral and more religious issues and experiences; that is, how to bring together fest and everyday life. In any case this is my own personal background.

I had been for some time involved in student theatre and in writing dramas and short stories when I encountered the political and ethical issues of Ernst Bloch and the religious and moral implications of the "theology of hope." The end of my own student period fell together with the European beginning of the student movement. In those days our more or less liberal ideas concerning ethics and aesthetics were confronted with political and social realities and with militant Marxist thinking which tried to find their new status beyond liberalism. But after two years of a more antiauthoritarian behavior and strategy the most powerful parts of this movement themselves created new authoritarian structures, lost more and more their connections to a liberating lifestyle, and set up universal ethical and merely political demands without showing how they could be realistically fulfilled. Increasing demands resulted in the increase of frustrations and aggressions.

This was the political situation in which Jürgen Moltmann published his essay on "The First Liberated Men in Creation" and in which I wrote my first small book dealing with the problem of how to realize an ethical as well as aesthetical existence. In a similar situation in the United States Harvey Cox wrote his *Feast of Fools,* which had to take into consideration psychological facts of personal and social identity and the present reality of civilization, culture, and counterculture. In this context I tried to give a reinterpretation of the gospel: the reality of the world as play of God, and God as the reality, the knowledge of which changes as human experience changes. In the main my essay was pleading for the need and the possibility of an existence which is at the same time ethical and aesthetic, arguing toward the integration of engagements in terms of social changes and religious experiences.

In juxtaposing fest and everyday life the following essay tries to concretize and illustrate this idea. Its basic presupposition is that it will make sense to deal with the *essence* of fest only in close connection with the *reality* of fest *and* everyday life. Otherwise an isolated theory and praxis of fest really can slough off fundamental conflicts of interests and real oppositions with a cheap reconciliation and a shallow enthusiasm. That is exactly why some political groups constantly tried to spoil ceremonies and celebrations of more conservative or even reactionary groups. They did not want to wear or appreciate beautiful masks before everything had been radically unmasked. But the problem is that those groups rather often are unable and unwilling to celebrate any longer on their own, or they only allow celebrations which guarantee a political effect. But I wonder if this is possible. I wonder if festivity is here not forced to become nonfestivity, indoctrination, and political reeducation.

In other words, I am convinced that there are sufficient reasons to argue against political programs which insist that one cannot be playful in the present at all, but rather seek only a better abstract life in contradiction to precisely the theories with which they intimidate their friends and enemies. Everybody has minutes of leisure time and night-dreams and daydreams. The question remains of how to spend them and how to deal with them. And so the aesthetical questions remain even for those people who are thoroughly involved politically.

In addition to this I would like to lay stress upon the fact that those theologians who rediscovered aesthetic and religious dimensions for church and culture, and with whom I deal and to whom I hope I belong, have been political theologians. That is true in any case for Jürgen Moltmann and Harvey Cox. They tried to correct an unbalanced theology of work, world, and engagement. They did not establish a new theology which eliminates these issues and which would dream its old or even new dreams in front of more or less psychedelic fireplaces. Quite to the contrary their new interest in play and festivity has been provoked precisely by universal ethical demands. On the other hand, as far as I can see, these theologians have been stimulated by the lifestyle of some "hippies" who knew how to celebrate without liturgical convulsions and without religious alienation, without semiskilled sentimentalities and without traditional meaningless rituals.

The second limitation of this book consists in the fact that its author is a theologian. Theological reflection, however, generally begins with the traditions of the church and the Bible, traditions which of course cannot be regarded as ineffectual, poor, and unimportant in terms of fest. That is why I deal especially with church celebrations and biblical stories. Theological reflections on fest need these materials, since they cannot be deduced immediately from philosophical theories or Christian dogmatics.

Christian people are used to referring to the Bible. Theological statements about persons and fests should also be derived from that book and not from universal terms or closed dogmatics. Dogmatics in any case can only be understood historically and has to be shaped anew by means of biblical material and by the challenges and experiences of the present. The Bible is a book filled with history and stories, not a doctrinal book. This means that faith expresses itself most of the time by means of stories, myths, parables, letters, visions—not by abstract terms. And stories and history cannot be transformed completely into a framework of philosophical or theological terms. Stories and history always manifest dimensions which cannot be assimilated to such terms. One can discover new aspects in retelling them in this or that way, in identifying with this or that person or situation, in keeping distance to this or that figure. When confronted with doctrinal statements, people often feel unfree. One can remain untouched by abstract terms. Stories, on the other hand, often give people a sense of freedom. They engage people emotionally; they invite people to new experiences. Doctrines can kill faith; stories aim at keeping faith alive and exciting. These brief comments point to reasons for and consequences of the second limitation.

There is finally and frankly a third limitation. This book does not claim to offer an exhaustive conceptual scheme of fest. It is intended as a contribution to the development of a theory of fest. This means that I am still on my way and hope that the reader is ready to accompany me to a certain extent. I will discuss certain central elements of such a theory, but not all of them. I have left out, for example, the mass celebrations of fascism and its demagogic functions. Although I lay much stress upon the relation of theory and praxis, I am not going to give concrete advice and instruction for praxis. I am not writing a fest-program, although I hope that this book might be helpful for all sorts of *magistri ludi*, for a lot of different people who are creating celebrations, ceremonies, and liturgies. It might be important for all of us engaged in such activity to know a little more about the theoretical implications of and the interplay and tensions between different elements of fest. So although this book is not a scenario, I hope it will be helpful for the stage manager and the producer of fests.

Finally, after having mentioned the limitations of which I am aware (critics will surely find more and worse limitations) I would like to make some more personal remarks. This book is the result of a number of lectures, discussions, and even sermons. I have had opportunities to present its material and discuss it with several friends and different people in churches and universities in central Europe as well as in America. I have greatly benefited from their questions and contributions, from their patience as well as their impatience. I remember with especial fondness experiences with friends and colleagues during the academic year 1973–74, which I spent at Union Theological Seminary in New York and Eden Theological Seminary in St. Louis. I would like to mention with personal appreciation my friend Professor M. Douglas Meeks of the latter institution. Our collaboration on the translation has given me the impression that the American version of my concept is more precise than the German original. Occasional changes in the text reflect certain slight alterations in my evaluation of some issues and a few paragraphs are added in order to expand the context of my argument.

If the reader is perplexed by the somewhat theoretical discussion of traditional theories in the first chapter, he or she should proceed immediately to "David Dances before the Ark" at the end of chapter Two and, in the severest form of perplexity, never go back to the first pages.

Tübingen   GERHARD MARCEL MARTIN
Summer, 1975

INTRODUCTION

Even Calvin said it: "The chief end of man is to . . . enjoy God forever." But we seldom enjoy our worship of God. We are seldom aware of God's beauty. What is wrong with the way we worship God? Why are enjoyment and beauty so often absent from our worship and our lives?

Recent theologians of play have explained the squeezing of enjoyment and beauty from our lives as being the result of Puritanism and industrialism. Protestant orthodoxy has reduced the religious life to moral and doctrinal instruction. All things religious are to be measured by their usefulness for the solemn purposes of life. At least in form, a similar consciousness has arisen in the modern technopolis. All life has to be rationalized according to its goals. Urban society has a profound faith in technogenesis, the process by which the city is produced by human work or by the increasingly autonomous technological processes which human beings have set in motion. Worship and work contrive with each other for the stabilization and control of life. Worship is reduced to useful service of calculated ends and work is reduced to the production of predetermined artifacts. Thus worship and work confirm and mutually determine each other. Worship is needed for better work; work is needed to make worship meaningful.

Gerhard Marcel Martin's book joins the debate of the play theologians about this fundamental dilemma in contemporary society and church practice. Martin's contribution to the debate is a messianic theory of fest. He intends to move beyond the theories of play that have been developed so far because he sees them as failing in the end to come to terms with the entirety of human life in urban society. Worship and work do have to be kept together if life is to remain historical. Play theories which seek solutions to the modern dilemma by eliminating either worship or work end up being either escapist or ideological. Martin proposes "messianic fest" as the comprehensive category which sets both worship and work in a humanizing context.

The context really is the decisive factor in the whole debate, claims Martin. There are theories which place fest within a context in which the whole of reality is affirmed and confirmed. These theories cannot criticize and transform the contradictions of the "workaday" world. On the other hand, there are some theories which simply stress the excess of fest as a means of liberating persons from the necessity of work and the structures of domination in an oppressive society. Freedom is often gained here by cutting off relationships with the official formation of society. The first type of theory wants to create an official ecstasy in tune with the whole of reality minus its negations; the second wants to liberate people from their repressions and oppressions without continuing a relationship with the official world of worship and work. These theories continue the dilemma on another level.

But if the context of fest is the totality of life, including its affirmation and its negations, then we can speak of fest in the broadest sense as "the enlargement and intensification of consciousness and life." Then fest can relate immediately to joy and beauty in both worship *and* work.

The boldness of Martin's messianic theory of fest is its consistent interest in fest as the transformation of everyday life. He is especially adept in appropriating important insights from the countercultural and human potential movements. But he is also sharply critical over against their lack of perseverance in changing the conditions which they often want only to escape. According to Martin, the only context extensive and intensive enough to bear fest as the transformation of everyday life is the messianic presence of God's kingdom.

Martin builds his theory of fest by pointing to the power of the gospel to create its own festive time and place. The biblical messianic traditions are taken seriously as being alive with the possibilities of liberating celebrations not only for worship but for the totality of life. This view of fest is at heart a dialectic between the incarnation of God in the flesh of society and nature and the suffering of God from the pain of society and nature. The ecstatic exuberance, ecstasy, and affirmation of Christian worship arise in the Easter Laughter from God's own creation and affirmation of life in our midst. Such joy cannot meditate in a corner. It wants to come out and express itself. But it is not a joy which causes people to lose reality contact with the world. It is a joy whose transcendence breaks through without breaking out of the world in which the cross of Christ stood.

This is not a "how to" book. Nor is it a book which is restricted to the practice of the church. But it is a book which takes seriously the deep need for wise and bold practical theology in the church today. Those who have a passion for a more faithful and liberating practice of worship in the contemporary church can expect significant stimulation in their encounter with Martin. Worship does not mean only spontaneity. Faithful worship should also be highly intentional. It must be thought about, prepared for, and practiced in the total life-situation of a community. Worship is easily ruined if this is not kept in mind.

Worship and work are both ruined when we separate aesthetics and ethics. The priestly tradition has always claimed that bad conditions make bad worship. Thus it has argued for the separation and purification of worship. But if the content of worship is aesthetics, it ends up in rapid world-flight. The prophetic tradition, on the other hand, has always claimed that bad worship makes unjust conditions. Thus it has argued for worship that is absorbed into the struggle for justice. But if the content of worship is ethics, it ends up in a rigid moralism. Jesus called for the humanization of worship so that in the context of God's grace the ordinary might become the kingdom and the kingdom the ordinary. Aesthetics and ethics are redeemed as they are taken up into the horizon of God's grace in which both Sunday and everyday experience the same grace of God. And thus work can no longer be understood as the automatic producer of guilt, and worship can no longer be understood as the coercive ritual for release from guilt.

Worship can also be ruined by happening at the wrong time. The utterly new thing about Jesus' proclamation of the kingdom is his announcement of the time. *"Today* this scripture has been fulfilled in your hearing" (Luke 4:20). The messianic fest can begin when we are living in God's time. If it begins before the presence of God's kingdom is acknowledged, the worshiping of the community will be premature and presumptuous; it will be nothing but an ecstasy which is blind to the signs of the times. If it fails to begin when the kingdom has come near in gospel, sacrament, and the "least of these my brethren," it will have begun too late. Then it can be nothing but a continuation of times remembered. Messianic festive time cannot be forced. It will find its rhythm and its modulations from beyond itself. It will be both out of joint with the times and patiently in love with the times. The joy and the beauty of worship and work will appear as festive time temporizes us according to God's history with his creation and his people.

M. Douglas Meeks

1.

TRADITIONAL
THEORIES OF FEST

FESTIVITY AS BEING
"IN TUNE WITH THE WORLD"

What follows is a presentation of some of the more significant recent theories of fest. Quotations from these theoretical frameworks will provide for a fair interpretation of the theories under discussion and will, in turn, occasion a consistent, objective criticism.

In his theory of festivity, Josef Pieper inquires about the most profound basis of and the real motive for fest and discovers it in the fact that "at bottom *everything that is, is good and it is good to exist*" (51, 20).[1] Therefore, "underlying all festive joy kindled by a specific circumstance there has to be absolutely universal affirmation extending to the world as a whole, to the reality of things and the existence of man himself" (51, 20). Pieper's core sentence runs, "To celebrate a festival means: to live out, for some special occasion, and in an uncommon manner, the universal assent of the world as a whole" (51, 23). This festive human "agreement with everything that is" (51, 24) corresponds to the words "very good" spoken by God on the seventh day of creation. God himself "affirms and loves . . . all without exception" (51, 35). Therefore human beings "confirm" in festivity the "goodness of existence by offering the response of joy" (51, 22). And that is why "affirmation is the fundamental form of Christian liturgy. Christian liturgy is in

---

1. Throughout this text the first number in parentheses refers to a work listed in the bibliography at the back of the book, and the second to a specific page in that work.

fact 'an unbounded Yea- and Amen-saying.' Every prayer closes with the word: Amen, thus it is good, thus it shall be . . ." (51, 28). "All worship is affirmation, not only of God but also of the world" (51, 28).

In time of protest and rebellion, whoever speaks of affirmation, of confirming the existing conditions, and especially of heightened confirmation, will be suspected from the beginning. Thus Diethart Kerbs sees in this concept of Pieper's a "paradigm example" for "reactionary and dangerous affirmative optimism . . . from the Catholic perspective" (33, 46, note 25) and recommends a thorough scrutiny of Pieper's model.

If one follows Kerbs's recommendation, however, one runs up against an argument which is more extreme than one with which totally suspicious critics might like to be confronted. Pieper guards against the formula "absolutely universal affirmation" being simply identified "with shallow optimism, let alone with smug approval of that which is" (51, 20–21; similarly p. 41). Rather, according to his understanding, in festivity the "hidden ground of everything" (51, 34), the "reality of Eternity" (51, 29) reveals itself; in cult "men hope that they will be vouchsafed a share in the superhuman abundance of life" (51, 29). "The celebrant becomes aware of, and may enter the greater reality which gives a wider perspective on the world of everyday work, even as it supports it" (51, 32). Finally, celebration of Easter means "mysterious contemporizing" of "grace" and "new life" (51, 37). It is only such *broadening* of the horizon which determines the festive certainty "that all is well with the world and life as a whole" (51, 21). Only out of this perspective can "grief, sorrow, death" be accepted, "and therefore affirmed as meaningful in spite of everything" (51, 22).

If one is fair with Pieper and more critical over against his critics, one can even find at certain places in the book the opposite of affirmation. "Of course rapture is always a shattering of man's ordinary 'normal' relationship to the world" (51, 37). And when the "true reality" is affirmed, it is precisely this reality which may be forced to appear by means of the crassest satire, *poésie noire*, and social-critical painting.

Nevertheless Kerbs's criticism has grounds. Pieper's full

agreement with Nietzsche's sentence, "To have joy in anything, one must approve everything" (51, 20), impairs the more judicious evaluation of Pieper noted above. Nowhere does Pieper make clear that precisely when one approves *everything*, concrete criticism of individual issues becomes possible and necessary. Pieper also does not reach such a *correlation* of affirmation and opposition when he allows satire and *poésie noire* in the realm of fest; even they should agree with the true reality in mourning its absence (cf. 51, 41).

How little the critical element of festivity is considered as a positive and constructive dimension by Pieper becomes clear when he sees in the festive "shattering of man's ordinary 'normal' relationships to the world" the danger of "both interrupting the orderly course of human events and opening them to question" (51, 31); and, as if it would be self-evident, Pieper states that only "during festival [should] social differences be abolished" (51, 52). Then, however, nothing is put into question; rather, concrete criticism and effective transformation in everyday life are rejected. Such a theory of fest stabilizes and affirms the given actuality too undialectically. If according to Pieper "grief, sorrow, death" should too quickly be affirmed as "meaningful in spite of everything" (51, 22), there arises the question, Is there no insight into meaningless suffering and the needless brutality of death precisely before the broadest, festive horizon? Do death and dying have no political dimension? The festive mood propagated by Pieper is in danger by means of the gloomy comfort of taking out of consideration the reality of meaningless and avoidable death—in traffic and factory accidents and in the political struggle for power. The result would be an increased inability to make clear distinctions between necessary and self-destructive, functional and nonfunctional suffering.

Whoever begins, as does Pieper, with fest as total agreement to the world has no understanding of the differentiated positions of existentialist philosophy (cf. 51, pp. 4–5, 19, 22, 42). Sartre, Camus and others have not fallen in love with the absurd, "fortunately or unfortunately." Rather they wanted to become engaged in living, loving, and celebrating, and thus argued that "the metaphysical tragedy of being" has no obligatory consequences "for daily practice," to quote an aphorism from Lec (38, 8).

Even more, Pieper has no understanding of theorists of fest who claim that fest is essentially excess, "submergence in 'creative' chaos" (51, 15). Pieper quotes Roger Caillois, who maintains that fest—like war—is a "time of excess": "The most drastic conversion and consumption of energies, the eruption of stored forces, the merging of the individual in the totality, the squandering of resources ordinarily carefully husbanded, the wild breaking down of inhibitions . . ." (51, 60). As terrifying as the paralleling of war and fest might be—we do fear the fascist aestheticizing of politics!—the theory of fest as excess does have important reference points in the reality of practice.

FEST AS OPPOSITION AND EXCESS

What is at stake also in this concept is an intensified life and a broadening and intensification of consciousness. But this is no longer conceived under the sign of affirmation but under that of opposition. It does not aim at the representation of a total harmony but at a breaking out of every situation in the world and society which is regarded as insufficient and too narrow. Sigmund Freud, who at this point should be merely quoted as a representative of this theory, formulates it in the following way:

> A festival is a permitted, or rather, an obligatory excess, a solemn breach of prohibition. It is not that men commit the excesses because they are feeling happy as a result of some injunction they have received. It is rather that excess is of the essence of a festival; the festive feeling is produced by the liberty to do what is as a rule prohibited. [22, 140]

The Protestant theologian Jürgen Moltmann in his essay "The First Liberated Men in Creation" outlines, among other things, a critical game and fest theory. He also is essentially dealing with excess, meaning, protest, and opposition. Games should lead to liberation with the intention of emancipation "from the bonds of the present system of living." Moltmann is concerned with the "distorting of the images of rulers" in political humor—with games, caricature, parodies, and imitations as "a means of emancipation for those who are burdened and heavy laden" (48, 13).

A more comprehensive theory of these functions of the festive day has been outlined by the Soviet literary critic Michail Bachtin in an essay, "The Main Characteristics of the Culture of Laughing."

> The day of celebration made the whole official system with all its prohibitions and its hierarchial limits ineffective for a certain time. For a short period of time life stepped out of its usual, legally defined and sanctified way and entered the area of utopian freedom.
>
> Laughing builds up for itself, so to say, its counterchurch against the official church, and its counterstate against the official state. [2, 32–33]

In medieval laughing Bachtin discovers the "victory over the fear of everything sanctified and forbidden (of the 'mana' and the unending praise of 'taboo'), of the power of God and of human beings, of authoritarian commands and prohibitions, of death and retribution in the beyond, of hell, and of everything which is more awful than the earth," and he regards this implicit "nonofficial truth about the world and human beings . . . as having prepared the new self-consciousness of the Renaissance" (2, 35).

It is Bachtin's strength that he does not isolate the festive counterworld of liberation and laughing; rather he relates it to the "official" truth, to seriousness, to the official church and the official state whose reality cannot and should not be playfully disregarded.

> We know that the people who made up the boisterous parodies of the holy texts and of the church cult actually accepted this cult and served it. . . . The medieval person was able to combine the pious attendance at the Mass with gay parodies of the official cult in public. The trust in the world of fools, the truth of the world turned upside down went together with true loyalty. . . . Medieval people participated with the same intensity in two lives: in official life and "carnival" life. Their existence was shaped by two aspects of the world: by the aspect of piety and seriousness and by the aspect of laughing. Both aspects coexisted in their consciousness. [2, 40–41]

Thus according to Bachtin's description of fest there arises "a mutual estrangement" of "both systems of life and thought" (2, 57), a "joyous relativity of each given order, power, and hierarchy" (2, 51). His theory of fest nevertheless has its starting point in "carnival," in the "world turned upside down" because it is precisely this world which includes the official one, whereas the official world isolates and secures itself through holiness, authority, seriousness, prohibition, and taboo against excess and ecstasy. "Carnival unifies, blends and weds the holy with the profane, that which is high and that which is low, the great with the insignificant, that which is wise with that which is foolish" (2, 49). Thus carnival becomes "the fest of the time which eradicates and renews everything" (2, 50). It brings together "in itself all polarites of change and crisis" (3, 53).

Against the isolation of the festive, official elements on the one hand (Pieper) and against a somewhat onesided emphasis on opposition and protest on the other side (Moltmann), for Bachtin "fest" means high-spirited, ecstatic, extravagant affirmation of birth *and* death, body *and* spirit, seriousness *and* laughing, liturgy *and* fair. In this way Bachtin is able to interpret from his perspective the order of the cult and the official world in their limited validity, and that means in their relativity and relationality to the unofficial world.

Pieper, on the contrary, regards the climax and the essence of fest to lie much more in the context of the official world of praising God, instead of laughing, and in the context of cult, instead of parody, and allows the total event of fest to appear merely at the edge, "a germ of excess" (51, 15). Nevertheless he tries to be close to reality in defining the essence of fest, for example, when he characterizes it as an event which leaves "no zone of life, worldly or spiritual, untouched" (51, 26). He illustrates this with the Corpus Christi day in Toledo: "High Mass in the cathedral is followed by the procession; a musical performance, military parade, social display and Exposition of the Sacrament" (51, 25). And he does not leave out the bullfight in the afternoon. For him, however, adoration and contemplation, the unending praise of God, has absolute preeminence over any form of laughing and excess. Who is right?

To some extent the difference in the theories of fest mentioned above can be understood from their different intentions. Pieper inquires about the *essence* of fest as the deepest *ground* for all sorts of fests, whereas Bachtin tries to describe much more the total event of the festive day, its effect and all its functions, and Moltmann is more interested in its concrete political function of liberation. Opposition, however, is merely the political correction of excess. Excess is more and different from intended political provocation and the attempt at emancipation. Bachtin's approach seems to come closest to the reality of fest—in any case as far as we know it historically. This is so because he does not, in opposition to Pieper, assume that the yearly official church cult is sufficient to define the essence of fest and that every kind of celebration that goes on in the carnival atmosphere outside the church would be only epiphenomenal. Rather he regards "fest" as the constant opposite and accompaniment of cult and popular amusement, sacrament and beer tavern, liturgical mood and vital high spirits, gravity of ceremonies and lightness of enjoyment. Every theory of fest which does not regard "fest" in this way as a total event which is extremely complex is in danger of becoming abstract.

FEAST OF FOOLS, FEAST OF ASSES, EASTER LAUGHTER

According to Bachtin, however, these two different worlds remain strictly separated, even though they appear spatially and temporally in close proximity. The more astonishing it is that in medieval times there can be found some fests which did not maintain this separation but overcame the sacramental and hierarchical seriousness within liturgy and hierarchy. I am referring to the Feast of Fools, the Feast of Asses, and Easter Laughter, whose traditions can be traced at different places, especially in France, up until the eighteenth century, and which within the new literature on fest have taken on a paradigmatic and symbolic significance (12, 3ff.; 48, 29–30; 2, 50). To be able to judge which theories of fest justifiably appeal to the Feast of Fools and the Feast of Asses, and what both contribute to a new theory of fest, one must eschew mere catchwords and deal with history.

The traditional time of these feasts was the end of December and the beginning of January, that is, the days of the pagan Saturnalia (whose excessive celebration is to be found attested even among the Christians as late as the eleventh century). Christians also appeared in those days in deer masks, animal skins, and women's clothes and became intoxicated (9, 651). There were attempts in the West "to bring this mischief under control by declaring the first days of January and here and there also the following days as festive days of the church . . . later by defining these days as a memorial of the circumcision of Christ" (9, 651). Since all these measures failed to restore the desired seriousness and the averting of pagan usages, the medieval church integrated saturnal freedom *into* its own feast days. William de Auxerre argued that the Feast of Fools would be beyond good and evil; though it is outside (*praeter*) faith, it is, however, in no sense against (*contra*) it (15, 573).

From the beginning, however, there were strict rules and decisions made by chapters about how the Feast of Fools was to be celebrated. Thus, for example, it was decided in Sens in 1444 "not to pour more than three buckets of water over the head of the leader of the fools in the vesper," whereas no one should be prevented from undertaking "additional ceremonies outside of the church" (15, 584). And the regulations of Archbishop Eudes de Sully of Paris (1199) say that the verse of the Magnificat, "He has put down the mighty from their thrones and exalted those of low degree" (Luke 1:52), should not be repeated more than five times (15, 574). This *deposuit* of the Magnificat is the main catchword of the Feast of Fools. Therefore sometimes it was called as a whole the *festum deposuit*. It used to be the fest of the priest, deacons, subdeacons, and choirboys. Each group of them selected on a certain day their own bishop out of their own ranks. With songs and processions they led him into the church and decked him with bishop's garments. After that he celebrated the mass quite often with parodies of the biblical lessons and intentional dissonances in the liturgy. So it happened that the patrons sat down in the lowest chairs and the choirboys in the highest. And the lay people joined the celebration wearing clerical clothes.

In this *deposuit* one can certainly discover biblical criticism

8

of the ruling class and relativizing of the bishop's dignity—God puts down the mighty from their thrones!—and at the same time one can discover the saturnal basic scheme: the exchange of roles between the predominant and the inferior, the memory of the golden age and its original status when everyone was treated equally. Thus on this day the servants had all kinds of freedom. "Among themselves they played kings and lords, went around dressed in purple and white togas, gave presents to each other, wore hats as the sign of freedom; they were invited by their lords and were served by them; in general they were allowed to do whatever they wanted to" (20, 161). But what was supposed to be outside of but not against faith, though against frozen church clerical hierarchy, again and again fell from official channelization, and attracted rebuke and threats of excommunication and inquisition.

> The clerics appeared in the church . . . not only in animal masks but also disguised as women, pimps, jugglers. Instead of using incense they burned sausage or old boot leather. Instead of the responses they sang dirty songs. Instead of the host they enjoyed fat sausages at the altar. During the church feast they also took pleasure in throwing dice and presented very unsuitable round dances for the pleasure of the audience. Even worse were the processions following the church feast. Young people appeared in the costume of Adam and sought to amuse the mob with indecent gestures and speaking! [9, 652]

> . . . some of them undressed completely. Then they sat down in wagons filled with excrement, were pulled around the town, and threw it at the people following them. [20, 164]

Less harmful and less excessive in comparison with this was the Feast of Asses, which probably came into existence through the isolation of one scene from the presentation of the gospel in the mystery plays. In one sequence of this play large columns of Old Testament and heathen witnesses predicted the birth of Christ, and finally in the main scene it turned out to be none other than Balaam's Ass who prophesied the Lord's birth. In the Old Testament this ass is regarded as a wise and sensible animal, in any case more sensible than his master Balaam who, in contrast to his brave grey companion, did not recognize the angel who stood in his way. However, in contrast to the Old Testament, the Lord did not open the mouth of the theatrical ass; rather, between its legs was hidden a priest who provided it with a voice (cf. 57).

In another variation of the Feast of Asses one did not adapt human language to the ass, but rather adapted oneself to the language of the ass. This happened in a mass memorializing the flight of the Virgin Mary to Egypt. During the mass a virgin on an ass was led up to the altar and remained there until the end. The worshipers responded not only to the *introitus* but also—together with the priest—to the *ite missa est* in the end with a threefold "hee haw," or substituted these parts with that cry from the beginning.

Finally it belonged to the Easter Laughter that ridiculous stories and funny allusions came from the pulpit with the intention of provoking triumphal laughter after the Lenten time of passion. In Toulouse, as triumph over the Jews who had murdered the Son of God who had, however, not remained dead, a Jew was boxed in the ear during the celebration. Once, as a chronicler tells it, it happened that "the brain of the poor Jew spurted out" (20, 181). Easter fun which may be less terrifying to Christians happened, for example, when a preacher said from his pulpit that "if there is any man present who rules in his household, and not his wife, he should lead in the singing of the triumphal hymn 'Christ is Risen'. Then there was a great silence, since no man was ready to lead" (20, 183).

Two points should be quite clear after this historical excursus: the Feast of Fools, the Feast of Asses, and Easter Laughter can be much more easily understood from a definition of their functions in opposition and excess than from the definition of the essence of fest in agreement. On the other hand they cannot be taken as ideal prototypes of fest or as a model of present practice of fest. Rather, they are first of all an extraordinary mixture of festive seriousness and festive high spirits.

TOWARD A NEW THEORY OF FEST

In summarizing the presentation and criticism of the theories which have been mentioned one can say that in a comprehen-

10

sive theory of fest one can neither regard its essence as agreement nor its function as opposition or excess in isolation; nor can one reduce or assimilate the one to the other. For every theory of fest which does not regard fest as a *total situation* which is as complex as possible turns out to be abstract from the beginning. The consecration of a church and the church festival on the grounds, carnival and fasting, Good Friday and Easter Laughter, Corpus Christi and bullfight, belong concretely to each other. They happened together on the same day and at the same place, sometimes simultaneously, as in the case of the Feast of Fools and Feast of Asses. If in this way excess and seriousness, agreement and high spirits go together, then the pivotal point and catchword for the total situation "fest" is neither agreement nor excess but the enlargement and intensification of consciousness and life, that is, an enhancement of life in every direction. The festive agreement plumbs unexplored depths. The concrete opposition wants to get out of the narrowness of regulations. The combination of festive agreement and festive high spirits enables new, liberating experiences with both systems of thought and life and shows their relativity and relationality.

Harvey Cox has developed his theory of fest from this enlargement of consciousness and life and from the concept of the juxtaposition of different systems of experience. For him, "festivity is a human form of play through which man appropriates an extended area of life, including the past, into his own experience" (12, 7). "Festivity, by breaking routine and opening man to the past, enlarges his experience and reduces his provincialism" (12, 12). It "provides the occasion for man to reestablish his proper relation to time, history and eternity" (12, 43). According to Cox, past, present, and future, having equal importance, should be related to each other again. Furthermore, the transhistorical, transcendental world should not grow pale because of a onesided interest in historical processes. In memory, festivity brings back the past without betraying the present; fantasy is creative, it shapes the present and anticipates the future. Both transcend that which is at hand, but neither loses the patience and love of the concrete reality. Both prevent

11

one from running amuck, merely retreating, merely staying in place, or merely fleeing ahead.

Cox's idea of juxtaposition guarantees a remaining tension, a "discontinuity," and a "piquant cacophony" (12, 131–32). He claims that new experience is possible only through it. For Cox, "juxtaposition" is not only a style of thinking but also at the same time a fundamental aesthetic principle and a maxim of a new lifestyle.

As far as Cox is concerned, he has to some extent merely added the basic elements of festivity, agreement, excess, and the resulting contrast, instead of bringing them together in a more systematic ordering (12, 22–23). However, just by discussing various relationships and isolations of these different elements, criteria might be gained for successful and unsuccessful fests. Thus one could not only (with Pieper) infer the misuse from the essence, but also the essence from the misuse. Festivity would always be spoiled when the enlargement and the intensification of consciousness and life would be taken back, hindered, or forbidden clandestinely or openly. And this could be very well the case even where one is confronted with single elements of festivity.

In addition to this I am interested in the fundamental anthropological issues of such enlargement and intensification. Together with this goes the question of whether under the present social and psychological conditions this concept can be realized at all. There is a real possibility that the well-known "one-dimensional man" is completely incapable of living in more than one system at the same time and that thus even the most beautiful fest would be nothing more than the elongation of everyday life by other means.

2.

HOMO FESTIVUS:
FRAGMENTS OF AN
ANTHROPOLOGY OF THE
FESTIVE HUMAN BEING

It is important for us that we are now and then led to the limits of the human, as was originally the meaning of fest. Its history can be divided into two great expectations: the wish to become identical with the animals and the hope that the gods will appear on the scene. [Ernst Jünger, 29, 378]

Andreas is both animal and god. As an animal he is hitchhiking to Afghanistan, and as a god he sits among gods. As an animal he goes to sleep in the Hotel Oriental, and as a god he has his breakfast in bed. As an animal he wraps a fur coat around his whole body, and as a god he disrobes and assumes his regal station. As an animal he tells that he once needed a quarter of an hour to climb up steps covered with ice. And as a god he performs a well-executed leap on the concrete of the city. As an animal he sniffs after pot, and as a god he sees the world.
Andreas is both animal and god. His father, however, is a human being. As a human being he sits at his breakfast table, as a human being he loves. As a human being he buys tickets for the commuter train. As a human being he checks his coat at the counter and puts the tab in his pocket. As a human being he sits in the theater and watches the life of human beings who are both god and animal. [Gerhard Marcel Martin]

THE ENLARGEMENT OF CONSCIOUSNESS

For a more distinct definition of what enlargement of consciousness may mean, one should distinguish, with the British psychiatrist Ronald D. Laing, between "subsanity" and "hypersanity" (36, 129). Less than sane is one who is not even able to stand the narrow experience of everyday reality and escapes into additional apathy. Life is reduced, the horizon contracts more and more, affects are impoverished. Psychopharmaceutics helps in curbing impulses, drives, and affects; it helps to reduce the psychic tensions and to keep a relative indifference toward oneself, others, and the surrounding world.

Subsanity also can be found where one feels satisfied by that which is recommended as sanity and happiness by politicians, advertisers, and educators. In this case one adjusts and relies on preshaped patterns of everyday life and festivity without any distance. The subsane person howls with the wolf called society. He meets the demands of a society geared to production, and therefore he can and may consume the products of this society. He accommodates himself to the criteria of health and happiness which are obligatory in the given society and corrects his misbehavior, his exhaustion, and his despair quite often with the help of drugs and hormones. If nothing works any longer he reclines on the psychiatrist's couch, and will be accepted again by society as a sick person and cured again by the very agency which could actually be the cause of his illness. In the end this will produce thankfulness and assimilation, but it has nothing to do with the enlargement of consciousness. On the contrary, it is a narrowing of consciousness.

If apathy and adjustment are kinds of subsanity, only that person can be called more than sane who does not adjust completely to the prevalent principle of reality but rather suspends and transcends it. The principle of reality becomes questionable for him, although he does not simply escape from it. He becomes aware of his own narrowness in everyday life and even in fest. Reality—and that which is construed as reality—becomes more reflected, more intense and impressive. The narrow experience of "reality" is corrected by a more comprehensive experience of the totality of being.

The transcending and enlargement of consciousness also means being confronted with the whole presence of self and world instead of fleeing from oneself and the world. It means, instead of being satisfied with oneself and the world, a radical turning toward one's experiences and toward the reality outside which wants to come in. The brain of *homo festivus* would not work any longer as a "reducing valve" over against an over-whelming amount of external stimulations and would not work eliminatively any longer in protecting him from being "over-whelmed and confused" (28, 22). Rather it would exceed qualitatively that conception of reality "held by a slightly drowsy, middle-aged businessman right after lunch" (6, 3), the highly developed form of consciousness with which we are unfortunately only too well acquainted.

Thus *homo festivus* would learn to wonder, to dance, and to be silent, would live without taboos and false regression, and would realize that he or she has a body which lives and dies. Where human beings celebrate, they realize fully and beauti-fully that the animals are their brothers and sisters and that they share with them their lot of mortality and finitude. Through celebration human beings also realize no less that they are the image of God. In Huxley's reinterpretation of ecstasy in the Middle Ages, enlargement of awareness would mean to come back to

> Saturnalian orgies at one end of the scale and . . . mystical ex-perience at the other. . . . Shrovetides, May Days, Carnivals—these permitted a direct experience of the animal otherness underlying personal and social identity. Infused contemplation revealed the yet otherer otherness of the divine Not-Self. And somewhere between the two extremes were the experiences of the visionaries and the vision-inducing arts, by means of which it was sought to recapture and re-create those experiences—the art of the jeweler, of the maker of stained glass, of the weaver of tapestries, of the painter, poet and musician. [28, 125–26]

If *homo festivus* really looks "upon reality whole" as Pieper wants him to (51, 5), and if fest really is taken as "an event" that leaves no zone of life, worldly or spiritual, "untouched" (51, 16), then an anthropology of festive human beings has to take into account a tremendous breadth of experience of human beings, God, and the world. If nothing can be—as it was the case in the three-tiered baroque world theater—"too solemn and too ridiculous," then to fest belongs the "most abstract and the most animalistic, the most cruel and the most ridiculous, the most subtle and the most vulgar, the sacrament and the ex-crement" (1, 51).

15

With all this, the term "enlargement of consciousness" could be misleading. It could cause the impression that the main point would be the brain without the body. To overcome this misunderstanding I use often the awkward term "enlargement and intensification of consciousness and life." For the same reason, I use the word "realization" and the verb "to realize," which means both "to make conscious" and "to make real." For increased awareness expresses itself in life, if it doesn't become sick; it has the capability for that and must find the opportunity. Impressions which cannot and may not find any kind of expression create unbearable inner pressures. Beyond that there are impressions which can be gained only by dealing with the expression and the life of other people and can sometimes realize mystical submersion and sacred isolation at its periphery.

A further misunderstanding in the term "enlargement of consciousness" can happen if it is viewed as an explosion and expansion into dimensions which are utterly unlimited and boundless. The next chapter should make clear that this is seldom or never the issue in fest. Rather, fest encounters the new though broader and different limits. It knows and appreciates radical finitude; it structures space and time anew instead of transcending them.

Fest offers uncramped self-encounter, self- and group identity, not despite but precisely because of the enlargement of consciousness and life. If I experience greater attentiveness and more intensive communication, then I will no longer have the harassing feeling that I am missing my possible and better identity, my very life. Rather, such *limited* enlargement can be very *comforting* and can calm the disquieting restlessness which may be only too well founded. There is something like an aesthetic reconciliation which is always more than "merely" aesthetic insofar as it is acted out and experienced in a festive way.

To summarize: the anthropological and ontological basic term of my theory of fest is a reality principle which is enlarged and open and not simply screened out. That is why the consciousness of everyday life and the experience of fest belong constitutively together. This basic assumption will shape the whole second half of this book. Nothing should be thrown overboard except the deadweight of dullness. *Homo festivus* remains faithful to the earth as something that can be finitely transcended. He is in search of higher stages of life and consciousness without omitting, repressing, or disdaining the basis. Therefore he doesn't fall into nonfreedom or euphoria; he does not underestimate the objective dangers and social threats and he does not overestimate the increase of festive freedom.

YES AND NO

Hypersanity creates a particular consciousness of narrowness. Successful fests make the unsuccessful everyday life unbearable; they don't confirm its narrowness but they cause one to suffer from it. Fests make one painfully aware of the limitations, armor-plating, and ritualizations of everyday life. It is precisely this pain—and not aesthetic higher spirits—which forces people to integrate the good experiences of fest into everyday life, and that means to contradict the unsuccessful everyday life not only in an extraordinary, festive way but also in an ordinary, everyday way. The new alertness enables and demands the concrete *no* to subsanity, the opposition and the action of greater sanity. A more careful coordination between agreement and opposition should now be sought after by means of some anthropological considerations.

Homo festivus agrees with the totality—God, world, and self —in his or her activity of cult and celebration; in contemplation one gets in tune with this totality. One cannot wholly contradict the totum without falling into a deadly contradiction of oneself, since one is merely a particularity of this totality. The effect of such a contradiction would be to satanize the totality or to make out of oneself a powerless satan, the spirit who always denies (Mephistopheles in *Faust*).

No one lives from *no*; no one can begin with *no*, not even with a *no, but* . . . . On the other hand, *homo festivus* is just as little the spirit who always affirms. Because of a total agreement he can and has to deny and oppose. Against Pieper I have already argued that precisely if one approves of the totality, then the criticism of individual issues becomes possible. The festive person does not say *yes* and *amen* to everything. And even if the Holy Spirit, according to Romans 8:26, helps persons to sigh, it does not mean *alas, yes*; rather it means *yes, but.* . . . In the *but* in these well-founded groans is hidden the active *no*. Whoever never says *no* but can only sigh is hopelessly ill, so ill that he cannot even say *no* to his own illness.

The universal dialectic of *yes* and *no* which Klaus Heinrich has dealt with philosophically and anthropologically (cf. 27) is true also for the theory of fest: when *yes* is not held in *no*, the *no* runs amuck, becomes self-destructive, and lacks communication and language; but *yes* without a concrete *no* is sentimental and without savor. Only *yes* with *no*, which interprets the *yes*, can be the salt of the earth. Salt burns in the wounds and makes one painfully aware of them. Throughout centuries and millenia the dialectic of *yes* and *no* was at work in cult and sacrament. Blessing and curse, confessing the true and denying the false gods, the plea for grace and the begging for forgiveness of sins, the denial of the devil and the confession of the faith were very closely related. Whoever can say only *yes*, and whoever tries to make *yes*-sayers out of others, supports a society without pain, happiness, and horizon.

If total agreement *and* complete opposition belong to fest, the deficiency of Pieper's attempt to define the essence of fest is that excess and ecstasy as those moments which enable affirmation without the danger of perversion are treated insufficiently, and the deficiency of Moltmann and others is that they do not emphasize enough that excess and ecstasy are possible and meaningful only on the ground of the affirmation of fest and everyday life.

BASIC TRUST AND COURAGE TO BE

If the necessity of the concrete *no* is emphasized sufficiently, one must, however, ask further about the quality of the *yes* which lies at the basis of the *no*. Is this *yes* merely postulated, abstractly demanded, or hypothetically set up, or does it have an ontological correlate, a correspondence in our experience of reality? The *reality* of the festive *yes* seems to me to be grounded psychologically in basic trust and theologically in what Paul Tillich calls "courage to be."

For Erik Erikson, basic trust means the early childhood experience of "an essential trustfulness of others as well as the fundamental sense of one's own trustworthiness." Basic trust is "a pervasive attitude toward oneself and the world derived from the experiences of the first year of life" (16, 96). This attitude, as often as it might come into a crisis, can be regained and reconquered. When this basic trust never came into existence because of a lack of love and the inability to love of those who in the first months of life constituted the world for the child, a damage has been done which can never be cured or turned into good. This makes clear that one cannot say that *the* reality, being in itself, would be trustworthy and would invite a *yes*; but *the* reality in itself is also not cruel and loveless so that over against reality one would have constantly to struggle through to the *nevertheless* of the *yes* (Ps. 73:23). Rather, the love of human beings, though it can be understood here quite instrumentally and technically in the framework of vitalism and mere biological needs as a drive to maintain and nourish the species, represents the world so that it is experienced as trustworthy, and an affirming attitude toward it is made possible.

These primary attitudes of early childhood naiveté are different from secondary attitudes of adults. Even then, however, basic trust is maintained, but it expresses itself simultaneously in new and different ways. I would like to interpret the *yes*-saying of the adult with Tillich's "courage to be" and with his idea of "absolute faith." This faith has no particular content; rather, it denotes the experience of the power of being, the experience of being accepted, and the experience of the subordination of nonbeing to being. This faith is the "existential acceptance of something transcending ordinary experience" (61, 173, cf. 175–76). It says *yes* to "being without seeing anything concrete which might conquer nonbeing in fate and death"; "it is without the safety of words and concepts, it is without a name, a church, a cult, a theology. But it is moving in the depths of all of them. It is the power of being, in which they participate and of which they are fragmentary expressions" (61, 189). If basic trust is an attitude of human beings which has been made possible by real love, it will be maintained and transformed in the faith of adults. According to Erikson, reli-

19

gion renews and confirms basic trust (cf. 17). Because faith and absolute faith have reached the "limits of tolerance of the inner-worldly objects of their trust," they must be regarded as the transcending of human conditions of trust (50, 106).

Basic trust as absolute faith can be disappointed; there are universal eclipses of God and personal depressions, neuroses, and psychoses which make every form of trust and faith, even the Christian faith, impossible. "Night comes, when no one can work" (John 9:4b). There is a narrowness, a condition of being turned in upon oneself, a total context of delusion, as the Frankfurt school of "critical theory" would say, which make impossible any *yes, but* . . ., any basic trust, or any absolute faith. This and only this is the end of any possible fest. But wherever there is still a *no*, an experience of being able to differentiate the given situation from a utopian project, a little hope, pain, or a contradiction, they are made possible by a *nevertheless* which includes a *yes* within it. This *nevertheless* does not make a great fest, but if enlargement of consciousness and life is the maximal category of fest, this *nevertheless* is at least the minimal category.

DAVID DANCES BEFORE THE ARK

And David danced before the Lord with all his might; and David was girded with a linen ephod. So David and all the house of Israel brought up the ark of the Lord with shouting, and with the sound of the horn. As the ark of the Lord came into the city of David, Michal the daughter of Saul looked out of the window and saw King David leaping and dancing before the Lord; and she despised him in her heart. . . . And David returned to bless his household. But Michal the daughter of Saul came out to meet David, and said, "How the king of Israel honored himself today, uncovering himself today before the eyes of his servants' maids, as one of the vulgar fellows shamelessly uncovers himself!" And David said to Michal, "It was before the Lord, who chose me above your father, and above all his house, to appoint as prince over Israel, the people of the Lord— and I will make merry before the Lord. I will make myself yet more contemptible than this, and I will be abased in your eyes; but by the maids of whom you have spoken, by them I shall be held in honor." And Michal the daughter of Saul had no child to the day of her death. [2 Sam. 6:14–16, 20–23]

The ark, a cultic object, is carried into *the* city which will be the capital of the kingdom, into Jerusalem. The ark is finally out of the enemy's hands. And David is enjoying the successful life: he is a victor in the name of God. The enemies are defeated. God has allowed everything to turn out well. There is tremendous thankfulness and joy, a festive mood.

Joy does not simply turn inwardly; it wants to get out, to express itself. David dances. Dance and play are ways of freely giving away oneself; they have a religious, sometimes even ecstatic and orgiastic character. David dances; God is present in such a way that David cannot but dance. He is dancing more freely and frolicsomely than his wife is ready to accept. She, who does not allow herself and others to be a voyeur, considers her king to be an exhibitionist. Before God and the people one should not abandon and denude oneself in such a way. This is an old law: according to Moses, the altar should not have steps because there is a danger of denuding oneself before Yahweh in the cultic performance of one's duties (Exod. 20:26). One processes in a measured and dignified way. One grows stiff rather than becoming loose. One puts on a character mask rather than exploding out of the narrow framework of the self-contained ego. One takes a stance instead of running wild. One turns into oneself instead of breaking out of oneself.

But David is dancing, full of religious ecstasy, instead of squeezing himself, as does Michal, into the windowframe of a narrow morality. David makes this his explicit program: I want to play, to dance, to be frolicsome and ecstatic before the Lord.

The General Superintendent of Berlin was concerned about proper worship. In the time of Luther, processions were reinstituted according to the church order of the prince. Choir caps and robes had to be worn again. All the medieval elements of a rich but external liturgy, which was not free of magic and superstition, appeared again.

But Luther writes:

To the honorable Georgio Buchholtzer, Superintendent of Berlin, my dear brother in Christ,

... thus by all means do go around also wearing a silver or gold cross and choir cap or choir robe made out of velvet, silk, or linen, and if your lord the sovereign prince thinks the one choir cowl or choir robe you are wearing is not enough, then by all means do wear three of them, just as Aaron the High Priest wore three robes, one over the other. ... And if your lord, the Margrave, should take pleasure in it, his royal grace may jump ahead and dance with harps, tymbals, cymbals, and handbells, as did David before the ark of the Lord when it was carried into the city of Jerusalem. I do agree very much, for things like that, if only *abusus* [abuse] be kept away, do not contribute anything to the gospel nor do they take anything from it.

And Luther claims that out of all of this

there cannot arise any danger ... to the Christian faith ... , for it is a free thing and merely an order of human devotion and worship and not the command of God, for the command of God is the only necessary thing, everything else is free.

Thursday after Andreae, *Anno* 1539
Martinus Luther Doctor[1]

Luther argues: dancing does not take away anything from faith. There is no danger to it; everything is allowed. But dancing does not add anything to faith.

Michal argues: dancing does take away something from faith —its seriousness, its dignity, its festive structuredness.

David argues: dancing really does not take away anything from faith but it in fact adds something: joy, spontaneity, and festive expression. David dances not only because the dance is "a free thing" (Luther) but because dancing realizes freedom.

Michal is not free; Luther is more free; David is the freest. David dances. David is *homo festivus.*

Who else according to the Old Testament is dancing and playing and living spontaneously and ecstatically? If one follows up the Hebrew word for "playing and dancing" throughout the Old Testament, one will discover there is "playing" before God. Human beings "play"; God himself "plays." The world is the ground of God's and humanity's play.

The Wisdom of God plays before God (Prov. 8:30); she who

1. *D. Martin Luthers Werke,* Briefwechsel, vol. 8 (Weimar, 1930–70), no. 3421, pp. 624–26.

exhorts human beings to be serious is playful and high-spirited before God. She plays, as I understand it, with God's possibilities before the creation. Redemption, liberation from slavery, can also be adequately described with the term "play." Just as we will be then like those who dream (Ps. 126), we will be spontaneous and ecstatic; "praise and joyful song" is to be heard again from Jerusalem (Jer. 30:19). "And the streets of the city shall be full of boys and girls playing in its streets" (Zech. 8:5). Play and ecstasy are things to be hoped for; therefore there is an element of fulfillment where there is playing.

Speaking about play and exuberance before God does not mean harmlessness and dull harmony. There always goes with it, as with David, the explosive, the excessive, the abyss, all of which belong to freedom. For instance, 2 Samuel mentions a playful struggle between the people of Saul and David, but what follows is the description of a real blood bath (2:14ff.). And in prison Samson has to "play" in front of the princes and lords of the Philistines. Samson is placed between the two principal columns of the festive house. He grabs them "playfully," brings down the palace with the help of the Lord, and buries himself and his festively assembled enemies under the ruins (Judg. 16:23ff.).

Michal is right after all? Playful activities really lead to chaos? They really break out of formal religion and morality? Yes: but David is in contact with a reality which Michal does not know and is not ready to get to know. David is a greater realist. He who enters the sphere of God, who plays and dances before God, is no longer sure about his religious securities and guarantees. David is a greater realist; he participates in the ecstasy of life and death, God and freedom. Michal does not know this dimension. This may be the reason that she does not participate in the passion of conception, labor, and birth. To me *this* seems to be the meaning of the last verse. She did not make a great mistake, but something was lacking in her. That is why "she had no child up to the day of her death." She is not punished because she criticized her king, but she criticized him because she did not understand anything about the magnificence of God and the boundless freedom and exuberance into which his creatures might enter.

FEST AND EVERYDAY LIFE:
MODELS OF COORDINATION
AND NONCOORDINATION

> Revolution is the changing of the extraordinary into
> the everyday. [graffito on a building in Cuba]

If the basic anthropological and ontological category of my theory of fest is an open and enlarged, but not rejected or omitted reality principle, then the relationship between festive time and everyday life has to become the starting point and criterion for every practice of fest and the theory behind it. Thus, following the discussion of the fundamental anthropological issues, attention will now be turned to "festive time," which I construe as all time which does not belong to the working hours, everything which is not "everyday life." Festive time satisfies the criteria which have been developed above and will be generally understood here as a qualified time which stands out against everyday life as more intensive, awake, and aware life. Such festive time is a human privilege, a human possibility alone, namely, the increase of freedom, joy, and distance over against the basic sustaining needs of life. Festive time is extravagance, open space, and free time for the secondary needs, only the awareness of which constitutes the "quality" of life. Festive time is the beginning of all humanity. Thus free time, Sunday leisure, holidays, and the special "fest" are to be viewed as one.

There are relatively simple schemata for dealing with coordination of fest and everyday life, to whose presentation and detailed development I now turn.

THE LACK OF RELATIONSHIP BETWEEN FEST AND EVERYDAY LIFE

Three models can be suggested which describe the relationship of fest and everyday life. There is, first of all, the possibility that there is absolutely no relationship between the two. In this case (1) fest is completely isolated from everyday life, or (2) everyday life precludes every kind of fest which would be more than mere continuation of itself. In model 1 the everyday conditions disappear from view with a resulting isolation of the aesthetic. In model 2 the ethical is isolated because everyday life no longer permits a radical breakthrough in the dimensions of consciousness and life but simply perpetuates itself without contradiction and ecstasy. "Fests" in such a society are at the most political-national and intend to stabilize the everyday conditions by surmounting them in a festive way.

According to Pieper, Labor Day is a holiday which has been declared as a festive day for economic reasons and which in its history has often enough been celebrated with additional work and military parades. The result is a completely artificial and antifestive festive day (51, 55ff.). It would, however, have to seem to Pieper even more antifestive that the Catholic church has not hesitated to Christianize Labor Day through the invention of the feast of St. Joseph the laborer and the feast of Christ the worker (cf. 30, 176). Given the fact that such a holiday is celebrated officially and not merely taken as a day free of work and as an orgy of consumption, it will turn out to be an endorsement and continuation of the given social achievements and accomplishments. Celebration becomes an affirmation. Fest becomes an affirmation of that which is intended and accomplished in everyday life. It has only limited goals and does not recognize the contradiction to the value systems of the given society or the need to transcend them. Even the most beautiful fest of one-dimensional human beings is a continuation of everyday life by other means.

Model 1—fest without reality contact with everyday life— does intend to realize values other than those of the society but has lost contact with everyday reality and its conditions. Everyday life is swallowed by fest and forgotten; fest withdraws into dimensions which are unattainable for and inaccessible to everyday life. The syndrome of such fest is loss of reality contact, illusions which do not take into consideration those who have no rights and are offended, those who labor and are heavily laden—even if one belongs to them! Aesthetics becomes aestheticism and becomes a substitute for political liberation. Then there emerges a sect mentality for aesthetics and pious meditators who are alien to the world, who, although they claim to be superior to the world and society, nevertheless lose their contact with reality in the depths of meditation and in the sophistication of their games. Cosmopolitanism ends up almost inevitably in an acosmic and apolitical frame of mind.

There is no question that the aesthetic belongs to fest; but if the aesthetic celebrates itself then there emerges the "art festival in which the works of art are themselves the occasion and the center of interest." Art isolates itself, and the arts make themselves free and independent in a problematic way (35, 410), as Helmut Kuhn argues in connection with the question of the meaning and the origin of art. Then fest is "raised so high above life" that it is no longer able to be "heightened life" which it "fundamentally and principally" should be (35, 403). In this context of the criticism of fest and aesthetics also belongs the false interpretation of Schiller's *Letters on the Aesthetic Education of Man* (1795) (cf. 43, esp. 164ff.; 44, 50ff.). The danger is that "an education by means of art [becomes] an education for art" (24, 78). In dealing with a work by Kuhn, Hans-Georg Gadamer has articulated this danger in such a concise and pregnant way that the passage in which he sets the "poetry of aesthetic reconciliation" in opposition to the "prose of alienated reality" should be quoted:

> In place of the true moral and political freedom for which art should prepare people, there appears the formation of an "aesthetic state," of an educated society interested in art. . . . The reconciliation of the ideal and life through art is merely a partial reconciliation. Beauty and art lend reality only an ephemeral and effulgent glimmer. The freedom of feeling to which they elevate us is freedom merely in an aesthetic state and not in reality. [24, 78–79]

FEST AS THE FUNCTION OF EVERYDAY LIFE

After the scrutiny of the models of the lack of relationship between fest and everyday life, the question of a false coordination of fest and everyday life presents itself. Model 3 expresses itself in this program: fest, Sunday, and free time are functions (very intentionally, and not just by accident, as may be the case in models 1 and 2) of everyday life, of its necessities, its loves, and its needs. Fest gains a *compensatory* character. Festivity replaces everyday lack and fulfills needs which cannot even be expressed in everyday life. It is a fest in which one tries to grasp what is denied in everyday life and will remain denied. The color and fullness of life in the festive dimensions of life reaffirm the colorlessness and deadliness of everyday life.

To the same program belongs the following procedure. Temporary slackening of regulated, rigid everyday life is useful precisely to make everyday life go smoothly. Such slackenings can be seen in the increased or even excessive consumption of what has been produced in everyday life. As Riesman puts it in his book *The Lonely Crowd*, ". . . the prestige of work operates as a badge entitling the holder to draw on the society's idleness fund" (52, 329). Such periods of intensified consumption, loosened regulation, and compensatory freedom can be grasped under the catchword "mores of venting," as a "regulated" licentiousness.

"Mores of venting are mores whose meaning lies in the *neutralization of accumulated tension* which might threaten the order of a group." Their effect is that neither the unity of the group nor the authority unifying it will be lost (7, 1220–21). Under such perspectives one can describe all customs of Mardi Gras, festive excesses, and so on, as an institution which regulates or ritualizes "the permanent social conflict." It allows politically exploited people to make revolution without actually making a revolution, that is, to "improve" periodically their social position again and again for a short time without touching the society's structure of domination. In such a way the reasons for social conflict are neutralized. "Of course Mardi Gras may set the world on its head for a few days; but in the long run *nothing* in the world is changed by it except that one loses one's head" (63, pp. 298, 303).

This way of dealing with tensions by neutralizing them is rather old. Already in the statement of the theological faculty of Paris in 1444, mentioned above, there was quoted and rejected an argument for the toleration of the excesses accompanying the Feasts of Asses and Fools. Their argument maintained that such excesses had been allowed by the ancestors "so that the foolishness which is natural to us and seems to be innate, comes out at least once every year. The wine barrels would burst if one would not open the bunghole from time to time and give them air." "We play the fool for a couple of days so that we can return to worship after that with even more eagerness" (20, 166–67).

I view as terribly flat this model 3 with its characteristics of compensation and mores for venting pressure, where all stress is laid upon the fact that all free time is a function of the time which is not free. A few years ago the Division of Health Information of the German Federal Department of Public Health published a brochure entitled "One Hundred Tips for Fun and Leisure." This brochure forces people to find fun in leisure, since everyday is without fun and will continue to be without fun in the future. "Free time," it says, "should be experienced more consciously," so that obviously one will *not* have to experience the work day more consciously and critically. Fun beyond work is supposed to "get one out of one's rut" so that fun comes back into life, since the boss will certainly not tolerate fun, and furthermore, life at work is and will remain a rut. In this way everyday life is not allowed to have chances of transformation and free time is glorified as a time in which "everyone [can] untie oneself playfully from everyday life." Everything is interpreted as "compensation for the professional everyday life." We must learn, it says, "that free time enables us to find compensation, relaxation, and recreation as well as physical exercise, all of which are missed in everyday life." Up to the final sentence, "Dare to play. Start immediately. It's never too late for fun. Free time is a little vacation," this brochure takes it for granted that "hard weeks go together with gay fests."

Finally, after it has been obscured that everyday life itself has a chance to be a special day and to become a fest, appears the lie that in the free time everyone "is allowed" to develop oneself as one likes most. First of all, I felt uncomfortable with the *is allowed*. Who is it who so generously allows this? And second, I do know enough instances which notoriously forbid one's behaving as one wants in free time. According to the categories of the play theologian David L. Miller, the whole concept belongs to the "Coca-Cola Philosophy" (47, 106). The *pause that refreshes* means that life essentially consists of work, but there are pauses in which you may consume refreshments. These pauses, however, are nothing more than interruptions of work, of that which is considered to be regular and really obligatory. The pause refreshes so that one can work better. But it is not even considered here that work is not merely the reproduction of life but can contribute to the production of a more humane life, to the free development of the play of all human powers.

There is a nonaffirmative variant of the program of "fest as a function of everyday life" with a pedagogical and emancipatory intention, namely, political role-*playing* and the "political vespers" [*Politisches Nachtgebet*]. Both shall be discussed in the chapter on the new practice of fest.

OLD TESTAMENT DIMENSIONS OF FESTIVE TIME

Models 1 to 3 are of course not immediately given but are mediated by historical processes in which the relationship between festive time and everyday life fluctuates or falls out completely. What follows is a short sketch of dimensions of special festive time and Sabbath time in the Old and New Testaments. Such a presentation can make sense only as a part of theological social anthropology, whose insights are derived from the biblical material, as I have argued in the preface. Such an attempt must deal with creation *and* fall, Old Testament law and wisdom, prophecy and rabbinic problems, the message and story of Jesus, the Pauline doctrine of justification, and finally it must deal with messianic hopes which are still unfulfilled and directed toward a new heaven and a new earth. This can be done here only aphoristically, but one must feel obliged to make this attempt if one is not to fall too quickly into abstraction and a narrow dogmatic frame of mind. I will begin with an interpretation of the Old Testament Sabbath.

The Seventh Day of Creation

The seventh day of creation is festive time. God rested on this day from all his works—not because he was frustrated or disappointed over humanity or his work, but because everything was "very good." Rest, nondoing, is a quality of divine life, in which human beings should and may participate since they are created in the image of God. Such leisure is not the beginning of all vice but the beginning of all freedom and values of life beyond production and consumption. Leisure is an achievement for gods and grown-up people. Plants and animals, even children, who do not live in secondary orders—and the distinction between Sunday and everyday life is such a secondary order—are not able spontaneously to rest in a festive or Sabbath way on their own; they simply participate in the rest of God and his image. The woodpecker industriously pecking on Sunday ruins the tree, itself, and Sunday. Cows and flowers also have no Sunday. The Sunday of plants, animals, and children is the Sunday of grown-up people. The horse's Sunday is the rider's Sunday. And the Sunday of the lions at the zoo is the Sunday of those who have free time and admire them.

What is at stake, as the Polish philosopher Leszek Kolakowski puts it, is "the recognition of the values . . . which cannot be reduced to the needs of physical satisfaction," which means the "triviality" repeated and emphasized by Jesus, that people do not live by bread alone (34, 38).

"Six days you shall labor, and do all your work; but the seventh day is a Sabbath to the Lord your God; in it you shall not do any work. . . ." (Exod. 20:9–10). Ernst Lange once called this day "the day of joy and delight. Life which doesn't relax, which is always only setting about to work, and doesn't open hands, eyes, ears, heart, and brain for receiving is quite surely not an obedient life" (37, 128). A recent collection of theological theses dealing with leisure time maintained: "According to the testimony of the Old and New Testaments, intervals for rest are justified not only for maintaining energy for work but they are meant to be autonomous dimensions of life." There should be developed "a specific ethos of leisure in which play and celebration will find a proper theological status" (14, 6).

All this might be right, but does the problem of the Old Testament Sabbath correspond completely to the problem of modern leisure? Are the structures identical? With this inquiry the broad generalization of all time, which is different from the notion of everyday life at the beginning of this section, becomes problematic. For several reasons the question must be answered in the negative; these reasons must become conscious so that the Bible does not too quickly and too naively become a recipe book when no one cares any longer about ingredients.

As the first step in dealing with the problem one must make a clear distinction between the Old Testament Sabbath and modern Sundays and holidays. First, if leisure is viewed as all time which is not consumed by vocational work, then it must be clear that there was no such separation of work and leisure in the primitive civilization and modes of production in Old Testament times. Life and its reproduction were more wholistic and happened with less structure and organization. If there was an ethos, then it was a collective ethos of the group or tribe. Our problem of leisure time, as far as more or less "passive" leisure behavior is concerned, such as relaxation and consumption of leisure goods, is not a biblical problem. Second, there are at best similarities of structure between Sabbath and "active" leisure behavior, such as creative hobbies, excursions, celebrations, and consciously structured free time.

Nevertheless Sunday and Sabbath no longer represent what they were once meant to be. In prepluralistic and preindustrial times they created a total situation for everyone; they were a delimited time under other rules. Today, however, the way Sunday appears is increasingly unclear. There are many services which must be performed also on Sunday, even including the services of ministers. For them, Monday or some other time must be considered their Sunday leisure. Thus "Sunday" usually can be found only as a more diffused, more unclear, more privatized, and at the same time, however, a more dynamic reality. But it no longer often appears as an actually delimited time, as a common situation, as a collective experience with a certain kind of social and psychological obligation. This pluralistic Sunday is much less, and in any case no longer officially, shaped by the religious establishment. But it is a free space for private self-realization or for political engagement of whatever ideology is denied or even forbidden by the constitution.

Finally one other possible misunderstanding must be cleared up: namely, it must be emphasized that the polarization between the holy and the profane is a modern one. Traditional religion gave a structure to the total life, including everyday or profane life. The working man knew himself to be dependent on his gods. The distinction between everyday life and Sunday in the Old Testament is the distinction between a life unconsciously and generally related to God and a life consciously, particularly, and exclusively related to God. One could say that it is a distinction between holiness and more intense holiness or, to quote Karl Barth, "God claims not only the whole time of man but also, because the whole, a *special* time" (3, 49). To be sure, from the creation narrative on there is an astonishingly active attitude toward the world, an attitude which is not impeded by taboos. But it is less self-evident that human beings are dominant over all plants and animals or that they are allowed to catch, kill, eat, and use them with a good conscience, in the freedom of those who are created in the image of God. Therefore they need an explicit permission from God (see esp. Gen. 9:1–4). And in this context the reality of sacrificial cults is very telling. They feel obliged to give thanks by sharing animals and fruits of the field with the Lord of creation.

If one wants to appropriate the value of Sabbath and Sunday in our time, one must try to interpret them structurally and existentially, taking into consideration the contemporary differences as far as cultural history, sociology, and psychology of religion are concerned. Then, and only then, can Sunday and Sabbath be understood as a time which is distinct from everyday life and which has its own character in the sense in which we described at the beginning of this section. But structural and existential interpretation of the biblical day of rest cannot be indifferent to the real history of this day.

In such a structural definition it is obvious that the question of a cultural origin of the Sabbath and its possible change of character in the course of history, as well as the question of the historical continuity or discontinuity between Sabbath and Christian Sunday as a celebration of the resurrection, should be taken into account. At this point, however, I will simply make a brief reference to Erich Fromm, who has attempted to interpret the history of Sabbath psychoanalytically as a process in which Sabbath, originally a day of taboo, became more and more a day in which taboos were eliminated and the primordial wishes were fulfilled. In his view, "the original character of the Sabbath was in no sense a positive effect serving rest and restoration but a negative effect which was defined by the renunciation of the subduing of nature" (23, 176). Only in the course of history does Sabbath as a day of repentance become Sabbath as a day of joy through the unification of the characteristics of both days as the day of reconciliation. The prohibition of work can thus mean "restitution of the paradisiacal condition without work" (23, 179). "The day of repentance on which people had to renounce work becomes a day of delight, of harmony between human beings and nature, which fulfills what originally was to be prevented" (23, 180). Thus only in the course of history would Sunday have become a positively qualified period of time, an intensified experience of life in comparison with everyday life and its limitations. The problem of regression, the displacement of wish fulfillment toward the infantile, will be further discussed later.

The Fall, Fratricide, and Prophetic Criticism

It is not quite clear whether the Fall and Cain's fratricide happened on a Sabbath or on a weekday. (This is not such an absurd question. Even as late as 1700 there was a discussion in Lutheran orthodoxy of whether the world was created in spring or autumn. This, however, was not a fundamental article of belief, so no one had to know the question, and its dogmatic answer was not binding and therefore could be denied.) As unsure as it is whether the Fall and Cain's fratricide happened on a Sabbath or a weekday, it is nevertheless clear and evident that both actions happened in the sphere of secondary needs which belong to Sunday. The first generation wanted to be like God although they had enough to eat; the next generation murdered not for survival, not for food, but for life, for religious reasons: Abel's offering is accepted by Yahweh, but Cain's is not. The denial of the assurance of grace compels a murderous aggression against the one who received grace. Because of secondary needs Cain is wrecked psychologically and Abel is physically lost. The universal curse which results from the Fall (Gen. 3:17bff.), is laid particularly on Cain: "When you till the ground it shall no longer yield its strength: you shall be a fugitive and a wanderer on the earth" (Gen. 4:12).

The "Sunday" that went wrong makes everyday life unbearable. Here leisure or the increase of the chance for humanity is in fact the beginning of sin. This resulting situation can also be made clear in the story of the Fall, which from the point of view of cultural history signals a breakthrough, namely, an attempt at the increase of life: to want to be more than the image of God, to be God himself, to learn the difference between good and evil, to "get out of the garden of the animals," as Bloch has put it.

Qualified time in the Old Testament was never again so radically distorted as in the story of Cain and Abel. But the prophetic criticism of political life in everyday and of religious "Sunday" is also varied, massive, and cannot be ignored. This criticism is directed against false politics as well as false religion; both belong constitutively together in Israel. If one is corrupt, the other is also corrupt. There is no true life in the false life. The prophet Amos especially makes this clear. In Amos 2–6, social accusation goes hand in hand with this accusation against worship which has become unauthentic. "I hate, I despise your feasts, and I take no delight in your solemn assemblies" (Amos

5:21). There follows the refusal of burnt offerings and cereal offerings. "Take away from me the noise of your songs; to the melody of your harps I will not listen" (Amos 5:23). Unpious offerings are useless (Hos. 8:4–14; cf. Isa. 28; Jer. 23:9ff.; Hos. 4:4–11; Micah 3). At the high point of the prophetic critique of religion not only is the Sunday that went wrong, as was the case with Cain and Abel, made unbearable, but both everyday life *and* Sunday are corrupted, and "Sunday," that is, liturgy, fest, and offerings, becomes empty and can rectify nothing.

As Israel becomes powerless on the level of power politics, the ritualized, meticulously observed, but rigid Sunday occasions a lack of love on a more private, human level. Sunday corrupts everyday humanity and by doing so distorts itself. Here Jesus appears with his practice and his understanding of Sunday.

NEW TESTAMENT SUNDAY

Jesus plays off Sunday as ritualization against Sunday as an opportunity for humanity. *Against* ritualization he claimed that the Sabbath was made for man, not man for the Sabbath (Mark 2:27). Jesus criticizes also the misuse of the religious over against the ethical. He relativizes Sunday by putting it into relation to everyday life. Sunday is misused and distorts itself if it allows less humanity than everyday life. Jesus sets forth a new human criterion for Sunday: "Is it lawful on the Sabbath to do good or to harm, to save life or to kill?" (Mark 3:4). This is a question, but only a rhetorical one, because there really can be no question about it. Jesus' numerous healings on the Sabbath are simultaneously provocative and symbolic. They are *provocative* because, for example, the sick man near the pool at Bethesda who was sick for thirty-eight years could have waited yet another day for his healing (John 5:1ff.), and they are *symbolic* because they are to make obvious that Sunday and the value of life, Sunday and health, healing of body and soul, belong together. According to Jesus' understanding, Sunday demands more humanity, that is, "healing." Everyday suffering is to be overcome by Sunday. "The blind receive their sight and the lame walk, the lepers are cleansed and the deaf hear, and the dead are raised up, and the poor have good news preached to them" (Matt. 11:5).

Of course Jesus' practice and understanding is only one particular aspect of his proclamation, not its pivotal point, not its center. The center of Jesus' proclamation is the urgent nearness of the kingdom of God. Where the kingdom comes near, Sunday is no longer the old one, just as the Old Testament laws of fasting and cleansing are negated. It is the message of the nearness of the kingdom of God that shapes all the individual acts and stories of Jesus and their messianic intensity. His reinterpretation and suspension of the law is legitimized by the intensive approach of this reality. His parables deal precisely with this nearness. His call for repentance is the call for conversion in view of this new liberating and surprising reality, and is not at all merely related to morality. The "changing of mind" begins with the senses and is not completed by moral sensibilities. Repentance, in its full sense, is training of the awareness for new reality and is more, something different from confession of sins or remorse or even a love affair with one's own failures. "Conversion" concerns the whole person, especially one's relationship to religion, to one's religious behavior, and thus also one's attitude toward Sunday.

What is at stake here is nothing less than a new quality of life before God. With, in, and since Jesus Christ, claim Christians, there is a new time, and in it a new human being, a new God, and a new world. The dualism of fest and that which is not fest has been overcome just as has the dualism between cult and the profane world, what is clean and what is unclean. Thus, according to Paul, service [Dienst] in everyday becomes worship [Gottesdienst] (Rom. 12). This cannot mean that joy and freedom of worship are forbidden or will be lost, or that they capitulate in view of the suffering of everyday life, but that they should penetrate everyday life as a ferment. Joy and freedom should not withdraw in a loveless way into the quiet corners of a world which pretends to be sane.

As a result of his expectations of the kingdom of God, John on Patmos had a vision of a new heaven and a new earth. God will dwell with all people; the heavenly Jerusalem no longer has a temple. This is the utopia of a world in which the distinction between the holy temple and profane space, holy and more holy, everyday life and Sunday, active and passive behavior in free time, no longer makes sense. It is the hope in a final reconciliation and mediation of culture and nature, of being a body and having a body. The heavenly Jerusalem is a city with concrete dimensions and limits. City always means culture. In this city live people from whose eyes the tears have been wiped away (Rev. 21:4). In this city which is no longer alienated from nature, "trees of life" are found everywhere (Rev. 22:2).

But we know only a very earthly Jerusalem; the vision of John is not present; the kingdom has not yet come in the way that Jesus expected it to come. But with Jesus a hope, an impulse, a driving power has come into this world. This means a breakthrough to a new world in which peace, love and justice will rule. Christians participate in this breakthrough; our practice of fest and Sunday belongs to this process.

MESSIANIC THEORY OF FEST

The only possible messianic understanding of fest is that everyday should become "Sunday" with the result that Sunday becomes "everyday," the ordinary situation becomes the kingdom of God. This, however, is and will remain a genuinely messianic perspective and can be realized here and now only in the signs of hope, incarnation, and the cross. For this reason the sense of reality and the utopian breakthrough belong together, as was demanded in the broadened theory of fest developed above. In such an outline Christianity is a religion which is utopian and at the same time related to the present, a religion which combines the realism of the human situation, the pain of the present, with the future of possible transcendence and joy. But hope and utopia never betray or supplant the reality of vocational, family, and social life and the reality of guilt, suffering, finitude, and death.

When the futuristic messianic perspective is lost, the formula "everything should be Sunday and fest" may still remain. Then the present is said to be the fullness of time. Hippies and some subcultures have claimed this in the last decades, but in doing so they have lost sight of the everyday conditions.

Apolitical meditation, ecstatic dance without end, and psychedelic dreams are symptoms of model 1: lack of relationship between fest and everyday life. There is in fact a basic mood of ecstatic trust and dreamlike optimism which no longer knows the pain, the spiritlessness in oneself and others, the sickness, the social misery, and the pressure of the whole suffering and groaning creation. It is precisely to this creation, according to Mark 16:15, that the gospel is to be preached. Not only current "critical theory" but also Christianity have to define "freedom" as a reality which is known not to exist anywhere so far. Precisely this is the "scandal of the qualitative difference," to quote Herbert Marcuse (42, 20).

Of course the sense of reality and the pain of the present can cause the messianic dynamic, which is also working in the present, to cease. Then there remains a dull melancholy, a rigidity of death, and a radical experience of powerlessness, a "worldly grief" which Christians, according to Paul, should clearly distinguish from the "godly grief" (2 Cor. 7:10) which is repentance and experience of pain in view of the unattained glory of God. It is the "grief" of the qualitative difference between the powers and powerlessness which shape the present and that dynamic which is working in the same present and which does not allow anything in it to come to a complete rest.

The theologians of the ancient church, such as Clement of Alexandria, Chrysostom, and Jerome, who spoke of an "eternal fest," of life as a long day of fest, were right in contradicting the love affairs with one's own failures and earthly despair (cf. 51, 23–24, 37–38). And also theologians of our time, with such reflections, may rightly interpret the Gospel's emphasis on the present, since it conveys a message which liberates and spreads joy. Pieper wants to speak of *everlasting* festival as existing in at least latent form" (51, 23). But if "the festive occasions did . . . exist continually and without cessation and were . . . so experienced" (51, 37), then this latency will be betrayed if it is not transformed into a real tendency according to the messianic formula: everyday should become Sunday.

Ernesto Cardenal, a social revolutionary and Latin American

poet whom one could hardly suspect of false and shallow romanticism, is impressed by cosmic rhythm and cosmic singing of praise and celebration. And although he knows the eschatological proviso, he wants to see in each of our days "an image of this eternal fest which has no end." "We have not yet arrived in the festive hall, but we are invited, and we see already the lights and hear already the music" (11, 142).

And finally, for the Taizé prior Roger Schutz, "fest without end" is not only a telegram from Buenos Aires for his birthday but an essential metaphor for presence, awareness, happiness, and friendship (58, 82). He seeks a deep inner festive joy and finds it again and again in himself and in others. Even the struggle may have the quality of fest, "fest as the struggle through which Christ becomes our first love; and fest as a struggle for downtrodden human beings" (58, 16).

If the Christian understands existence at once realistically and messianically he will not succeed in experiencing the festive character of the present as Greek harmony—even Pythagoras called life a fest (51, 38)—nor as the Stoic serenity and resignation of late antiquity. "In the festive ode . . . humanity celebrates the serene acceptance of the limits which are set to human yearning and life," as Godo Lieberg interprets an ode of Horace. "The invitation to the fest as an appeal to the right attitude of the soul and manner of living, the fest itself as verification and confirmation of *sapientia,* this is the basic thematic of Horace's fest poetry . . ." (40, 413).

If one has agreed upon the misunderstandings of the formula "everyday life should become Sunday," one has then to deal further with the positive understanding of this messianic fest theory. But before going on to individual questions, what it means to say that the messianic perspective is possible only in the sign of incarnation and cross must be theologically clarified.

"Everyday should become Sunday" means that freedom and joy increasingly penetrate everyday life, that they permeate it like a ferment. The quality of Sunday should enter into everyday life, thus even into the suffering and the toil of labor. That would mean concretely the greatest possible reduction of working hours and the humanization and eroticization of work.

Work can be done with more pleasure and satisfaction if it is a more meaningful, more purposeful and more rational metabolism in harmony with nature. Under different economic and social conditions daily useful actions and interactions can be more pleasant and step by step lose their character of coercion and alienation. That in this way everyday life becomes Sunday can be understood only as a process in thought and life, and precisely this process is the continuous realization of the incarnation. Incarnation here means that God is realized and appears in flesh, even in the flesh of society and nature, and that the consciousness of God and the quality of Sunday appear in the profane. God appears totally in the world instead of everyday life flying toward heaven according to the generally religious, but not at all Christian, scheme. If this is the direction of incarnation (God into everyday life), then the danger of failure and the reality of the cross are near.

The cross is the sign and the reality of him who out of love allowed himself to be driven to it. Jesus' cross was the consequence of his way of living. The cross was the punishment of those who were unable to tolerate Jesus, the one who infected them with love and caused disturbance. Christian theology knows and confesses such a love which might lead to the cross, and it tries to discover this pain in the depth of God himself, in whom it will be overcome. But the cross is not the main issue; it may be, however, the unavoidable consequence of the main issue. The main issue is the incarnation; this is the basic thought and basic reality which are intended in Christianity. Thus, passion is the consequence of Christmas, simultaneously the highest point and the turning point of God becoming man. That would mean that the cross is an unmistakable sign that this incarnation happens in a Christian way. "Cross" then does not mean the glorification of weakness, suffering, and the eclipse of God; it is not a symbol for resignation and powerlessness. It does not transfigure anxiety, blood, or tears into Christian guiding images. It is only the sign of the fact that love can result in suffering, that love may provoke resistance and can lead to the cross. In this understanding the cross is not the end of all love, but the sign of the struggle for the sake of love. The cross is the final consequence of the incarnation as realization of God in the world.

If this coordination of everyday life and festive time really happens in the sign of the cross, happiness, freedom, *and* pain will increase *at the same time*. The Christian cannot recommend happiness and the increase of happiness without realizing that whenever happiness is increasing, also pain, the experience of suffering, and resistance will increase. Alternative "experiences of Sunday," the increase of happiness and freedom, make everyday life less bearable and bring with them new pain. As I argued above, precisely this pain and not just aesthetical high spirits impels people to integrate the positive experiences of Sunday into everyday life. This pain also presses them on to permeate the limits of the freedom of everyday life with the freedom of fest as much as possible, and by doing so, to dismantle these limits.

4.

BUILDING MATERIALS

This chapter will turn out to be more aphoristic and less balanced than the preceding chapters. Thus longer quotations are brought together almost in the fashion of a collage. The following are critical remarks and programmatic ideas about the present practice of fest and about fests which might be celebrated in the future in the horizon of the messianic theory of fest. In all this I do not want to become an ideologue of a particular way to celebrate or a prophet of culture, who usually overdraws his account. Modesty is as appropriate here as is pragmatism. So this chapter intends to be a contribution to the developing theory of fest and to its present practice; not more than that, but not less either.

FESTS OF POLITICAL AND APOLITICAL
ANTIAUTHORITARIAN GROUPS

What we have argued for day in and day out has come to be true: there is really *no* border between "art" and "life"; the permanent creative process of life as art actually happens on the base of the mass. [Jean Jacques Lebel commenting on May 10, 1968 in Paris]

There is one anarchistic-antiauthoritarian approach to fest, already mentioned above, which seems very close to the program of "fest into everyday life/everyday life as fest." The apologists of this way, however, are quite often too optimistic and do not pay enough attention to the effectiveness, the actual political effect, of their dramaturgies of fest. Often they too quickly and too globally claim to discover in political demonstrations and street-fests a happy mediation between a purely aesthetical value and a politically functional value. They would too facilely combine playful and agonistic elements, or they would even claim that the borders between art and life are totally suspended (cf. 33, 34ff.; 44, 57–58, 67ff.; 54, 239ff.). In contrast to a political aesthetic which aims at certain goals from the beginning, the basic idea of this movement is: to continue to play, to celebrate, and to meditate. Life should explore all possible ways of expression and impression. The only ultimate limit this movement sets is that it does not allow festive acts finally to negate a possible correlation to political and social everyday life. So it is claimed that aesthetic and religious experiences can shift into concrete engagement. Fest, however, should always be more than agitation and provocation; fest should not be reduced to mere critical political engagement.

I am convinced that there should be a clear evaluation of such aesthetical-political activities, which really are provocations and calling cards of a new lifestyle. To quote Kerbs, they often are "prepolitical"; but precisely as such they are able to create "in many people that sensibility . . . which makes possible a politicization without reversion to a kind of fascist practice" (32, 46). Such festive activities are, as Kerbs argues in another context, actions of "political enlightenment and raising of consciousness," the "beginning of a learning process. . . . Whether in the long run, however, this process will strengthen or weaken the ruling system, has to be tested" (33, 37–38). In any case, even for those who try to mediate fest and everyday, this mediation succeeds usually only in a fragmentary way, if it does not actually deteriorate into something like the "arts and crafts" of revolution. For the great majority of those who got involved in political happenings (even in the building of barricades in Paris in May, 1968), in demonstrations with dancing and candy, songs and flowers, an atmospheric change happened which was clearly limited in time and space—a community of fate for one night in the battle against police, blood, and tears. But can that be called a fest? Or a fest of destruction? In any case it is a temporary high-pressure area whose subjective function of release should not be rejected out of hand (cf. Jean Jacques Lebel's report about the night of May 10, 1968). One really should not underestimate such functions. Jokes

and parody, derision and laughter about the rulers, as Moltmann recommends them in his "First Liberated Men in Creation," may be needed in certain situations and may have an
immediate liberating effect. But to me a fest seems to be more
than and something different from a caricature or a parody.
Furthermore, whenever caricature and parody become public
and political they can turn out to be deadly.

> The power of the powerless lies in such liberations from fear, in
> their laughter at the expense of deified rulers who are nothing
> after all but dolled-up dwarfs. People who are no longer afraid
> —yet who is really not afraid?—can no longer be ruled with
> ease, although of course they can be shot. [48, 14]

For me this is the most radical and at the same time the most
puzzling statement in Moltmann's concept. Even the *possibility* of having no fear is ironically relativized as soon as self-
evidence of its deadliness is stated. Not until there is a sane
world will one be able to live without fear. Here and now,
however, radical atmospheric change can mean the end of every
atmosphere, a total vacuum. This is in fact the final horizon of
the antiauthoritarian playful program of "fest into everyday
life." It proves the seriousness of this concept.

In this context one should mention still another political and
pedagogical concept of fest according to which groups start reso-
lutely with social realities and allow themselves and others only
those fests and games which with well-aimed certainty and pre-
programming end in concrete changes. Then fantasy and
ecstasy are controlled from the beginning and are not allowed
to overlook the real possibilities and realities at hand. Rather,
fantasy and ecstasy are meant to provoke and evoke alternative
experiences and alternate decision-making processes. Thus
aesthetics in general, play and games, fantasy, and even meditation become tools and strategical means. Some theater groups
work on this level; by playing before and with people they want
to confront them with the contradictions of the capitalist society
and to activate them to collective social activities. We can see
one group, for example, which has done this in Germany (19).
And though this parallel may be surprising at first glance,
some new forms of political "night prayers" and political wor-

ship and meditative exercises have as their main function and goal the informing of people and the discussion and preparation of specific actions.

In comparison with the programs mentioned so far, there are considerably more harmless and unpolitical ways to celebrate. Many antiauthoritarian fests do not realize anything more than the dissolving of the rationality of everyday. They amount to exercises of loosening in the context of having no context. Such exercises at most make the tensions of everyday tolerable, but they do not create a playful and festive countertension. This criticism is applicable to many middle-class parties with their small releases and harmless jokes. In these parties it sometimes seems as if members of a social class apologize during a whole evening for their own situation, without even themselves noticing what is going on. What could be a genuine step toward liberation and an exercise in more successful communication and interaction is spoiled and becomes idiotic "fun" with senseless and cramped gestures. And if the party develops properly, at about midnight there will be a reflective period for mutually affirming the inability for creativity and fantasy. The result is often a ritual of impotence.

Many people try to prevent this by trusting in new exercises of fantasy and creativity or in new ways of prelogical, unlogical, or whatever other ways of thinking and association. If experiments in communication and release of aggressions fail, the participants often bring each other to the do-it-yourself psychocouch. These off-the-cuff activities with playful short-therapy and instant creativity, with psychedelic colors and toilet paper, are most of the time merely ineffective playground activities. They do allow some dysfunctionality and harmless disobedience, which at most hurts the administration of a retreat center (and this may be a political result!). But all in all they are exercises of loosening without fest and new certainties. They are more or less higher forms of everyday relaxation without new festive countertension—if they are not regarded and designed as steps on the long way toward a new lifestyle.

According to my own experiences and observations, this criticism is also true for some streams within the "human potential movement" and the "personal growth" programs. In brief workshops in which hippies, psychologists, housewives, actors, and businessmen are brought together there emerges easily the danger of emotional overheating (that is, creating emotions which are lacking in life), antiintellectualism, ignorance toward political and social issues, and commercialized bourgeois counterculture. Laying all stress upon personal choice, as often happens in the human potential movement, ignores the fact that *my* choice—and especially the choice of prisoners, draft resisters, slum dwellers, and other minorities—is defined by the lobbies and power structures of a given society and cannot be redefined in merely personal ways. Dealing with social issues solely within the individual will result in either adaptation or withdrawal. Liberating people cannot only mean encouraging them to choose to live intensively, but at the same time must mean to change politically and socially the parameters of their choices.

I do not want to be misunderstood. I do emphasize the importance of personal growth and of personal liberation. I am very suspicious of people who constantly postpone their own problems and even their own lives by transpersonal, social, political, and intellectual activities. But I still have the feeling that too many people in the human potential movement are not sufficiently aware of the problems of transference: how to succeed in liberating the private *and* the social areas of life. Only then would life really become fest! How are the private and social spheres related to each other? How are we to find, within a pluralistic and antiauthoritarian approach, group symbols and ideas, even new kinds of rituals which liberated people can share and celebrate, instead of finally helping only each separate individual to meet his or her deepest experiences and life strength? "God"—as well as "final aims"—is "between you and me," as the Old Testament often puts it. God is *our*, not *my* God.

Nevertheless the critic should be careful not to be applauded by the wrong side for his criticism of various antiauthoritarian and human potential movements. For this "wrong side" intends to defame totally those actions and passions I have just mentioned by blaming them for regression, the return to the infantile. But there actually happens in these attitudes a suspension of wrong taboos, of additional suppression, of that pressure for efficiency which cannot be rationally defended any longer. Many critics on the wrong side fear every attempt to go beyond the socially obligatory reality principle. But it is quite possible that the fulfilling of wishes on the infantile level—if this is understood as only *one* step and does not isolate itself— can create a common emotional ground between adults and may liberate them from their adult isolation which reveals itself in ideological struggles and in the inability to cooperate. It may be one step in the liberation to common actions.

This does not mean that those who cannot work together politically any longer should now at least play with each other. Also the *forms* of regression must be further discussed. But it may very well be that in taking a step backward together—just as in certain kinds of processions in which people go two steps ahead and one back—in the end one really has proceeded. If one has realized and become reassured in the fact that he or she shares with other adult human beings innocent, childlike, basic human needs, experiences, and ways of expression, one can better tolerate the adult differences and will not absolutize them. Then one does not identify oneself or others exclusively by programs and political strategies—nor by programs of psychotherapy or creativity. Furthermore, one is not constantly anxious to convince oneself and others that the only form of communication is determined by the inability to communicate in any other form. That is why changing some patterns of behavior, emotional reeducation, and relief of tensions through methods such as those of "the human potential movement" can make sense and might be helpful.

LIFE AS COLLAGE

The technique of collage is the systematic exploitation of the coincidence, which happens by chance and is artificially provoked, of two or more realities, whose essences are alien to each other, on an evidently inappropriate level—and the spark of poetry which leaps across when these realities come close to each other. [Max Ernst]

In the first section of this chapter I have spoken against the tendencies to defend every form of festivity and dysfunctionality by claiming that it is immediately effective for and compatible with everyday life. Rather one should admit the unavoidable separation of festive time and space. This is true also when this separation is accompanied by the hope for a present-eternal fest. To be sure, fest should have an effect on everyday life, but precisely then it will remain a symbolic *as well as* actual realization of that which might be possible. In any case, in our society, those who might have been with the flower children on the "playground" will the next morning sit in their offices with tie and collar, and the flower children themselves may be clerks in a seed shop. Though there was a medieval cultural wholeness, as was pointed out above, the rhythm of fest and everyday life and of seriousness and high spirits within the fest has been a matter of fact throughout the centuries. Should not this rhythm be needed all the more in a pluralistic society?

On the other hand, the discontinuity between fest and everyday life should not be extolled as an extraordinary virtue. By doing so one is tempted to introduce the doctrine of the two kingdoms, to separate the causality of Sunday from that of everyday life, and to live in two worlds without realizing what these two worlds have to do with each other. I see this danger in the anthropological concept of "life as collage," as American play theologians have introduced it in recent years.

In another context Cox's idea of juxtaposition has already been mentioned. With it Cox aims at the remaining tension between the different elements which have confronted each other. So he approves of the "discontinuity," the "piquant cocophony" (12, 132). Only by means of these elements is new experience possible; only the "disrelation" breaks through boring, dead continuity, sets free areas for fantasy and increase of awareness, and effects a "creative friction" (12, 133).

Sam Keen wants to rediscover and defend the wonderful experience of the world in childhood as it emerges in the archaic-Greek and the Jewish-Christian era. He hopes to find a new balance between *homo faber*, the working human being, and *homo admirans,* the wondering and admiring human being. Contemplation and responsibility, the experience of basic trust and political action, together should create a new happiness which has been rarely achieved so far. The role that "juxtaposition" plays for Cox is for Keen the "polychrome existence" and the "principle of oscillation" (31, 194). It is *homo tempestivus* who lives an authentic life; he knows how to live the "economy of the seasons" (31, 197), as the Preacher in the Old Testament teaches. In this sense "the wise man is a dancer" (31, 198) who responds to the music of the situation with his own rhythm of life.

What is right and important in these programs is the insight into the remaining tension between ethical and aesthetical existence, between fest and everyday life. It is also right that awareness and awakening will be found mostly at the boundaries, in transition from one situation to the other. The reality of one sphere makes the other sphere alien. Only as a passenger between societies, situations, and levels of consciousness will I become aware of my own situation, will I realize its limits, possibilities, defects, and chances.

But who is able to live such a discontinuous lifestyle? Who achieves such "sliding identity" (Reimar Lenz), besides artists and a few free or liberated persons within a society which as a whole is full of coercion? Who can realize such different centers of gravity and different ways of life? Does that not reach the border of self-destruction and of notorious unfaithfulness over against oneself and those with whom one is related in love? A free and happy life goes together with a personal, social, and religious steadiness of one's own ego, however often and intensively it might "dance" (cf. 44, 30).

If the shift in media, the collage of life, is to be more than just an attraction or a spectacular event, there must be a center of the ego which makes one become aware of extremely different kinds of consciousness and of various tasks and experiences This demand does not correspond to the idealistic ideal of personality, to a stage-management of one's self, or to work on one's own profile, which in any case will lead most of the time only to a more intense neurosis of profile. But it does correspond to the fact that human beings cannot live in a human way in a wild collage, but rather only in contexts of understanding and meaning. According to most schools of psychoanalysis, every form of liberation and emancipation goes together with a strong ego, which brings together the demands of one's own life and one's own soul, the demands of one's drives and one's own biography; it directs them, integrates them, and mediates them with those of the society. This does not happen at the expense of the possibilities of life and development or at the expense of vitality, but only this makes possible development, vitality, and a new lifestyle which can test itself and will be conscious of itself.

Even the most spectacular experiences which fathom the depth of human life can grow pale. The Dutch psychotherapist G. W. Arendsen Hein, who came "out of the psychedelic treatment . . . blessed, filled up with the energy of life, with the sense of initiation into religious life," reports that this does not mean automatically the radical change of life or the transformation of the person; what really counts is only the integration of this experience into the practice of daily life and love (26, 102). Again, this integration is only possible for a strong ego. It is of course possible to live two or three lives at the same time—as a judge who has written his doctoral thesis, as a creative jazz musician, and as a practicing husband. One can succeed in doing this without intolerable ignorance or lack of passion for one or the other field of life, without permanent excuses, a perpetual bad conscience, and false compromises. But it is also true that such a person needs a strong ego, must have a rhyme for his or her existence, and must be able to blow a life-melody for himself or herself and his or her friends in order to be able and make others able to dance.

To summarize: the lifestyle of juxtaposition alone is not enough. It does not contribute to emancipation. On the contrary, it dangerously increases the commonly found weakness of the ego in an authoritarian society which is regulated by and lives in conformity to consumption demands and the media. People who truly want to realize new forms of community and radically different values will of course not be accepted or made welcome by this society. A subjective-political, reflexive-active, realistic-fantastic lifestyle is not possible if one merely juxtaposes fest and everyday life, social reality and fantastic possibility, and simply waits for the creativity (or destruction) within the juxtaposition to express itself. Such a lifestyle is possible only if one becomes aware of it, only if one reflects and corrects its processes, experiences, frustrations, and promises as the need arises.

In any case, in a genuinely human society the lifestyle of juxtaposition would not be primarily the problem of the individual, but rather that of the constitution of the total society (as Cox would agree). It is society which should be able to nurture different emphases—the mystic and the militant. It should do this, however, never to create absolute or exclusive alternatives, but so that not everybody has to act out and to live everything and the same things. Otherwise the program of juxtaposing mysticism and militant activity, as Cox has designated it, will break down because of an expectation of efficiency which cannot be realized.

Finally, the ego's power of integration corresponds to a power-field and a context of meaning in which and by which the ego integrates single discontinuous experiences. This is less an anthropological than a religioontological criticism of the concept of life as a great collage. The collage is only familiar with experiences of reality which are separated from each other. At most it is familiar with the "spark of poetry" which might leap across when these realities, which are essentially alien, approach each other. The life with the power of integration, however, is ready for the struggle between realities; it asks for authenticity and the quality of the given experience. Then fest and everyday life do not stand one beside the other as two finite experiences with the same value, but everyday life might appear as a reduced, narrowed, noneveryday life. The greater cosmic, festive, messianic reality is not without context; rather, it is precisely this reality which makes available the courage and high spirits to break through everyday life toward its messianic horizon. Only if the struggle between realities is understood in this way do enlargement and intensification of consciousness and life avoid the suspicion of being nothing but absurd acrobatics of transcendence, attempts at going down to the depth or climbing to the heights in a mood, and with the results of Sisyphus. Otherwise such attempts would merely artificially introduce everyday life on a higher level.

It is, however, just the other way round. Because the greater reality can be approached, one becomes painfully aware of the narrow reality and at the same time of the possibility of transcending it. From this perspective the message of the nearness of the kingdom of God means nothing else.

NEW PRACTICE OF FEST AND COUNTERCULTURE

It should be clear that everything that happened in this historic night was completely improvised: no leadership, no preparation, very little coordination. It was a spontaneous explosion. [Jean Jacques Lebel commenting on the night of May 10, 1968]

Rolf Schwendter states:

The new fests . . . remain all too close to the middle-class party: as a mere negation of rituals, as the absence of structure, as if the structure of a society with domination would not have to be essentially much more complex than that of a vertical society. [59, 255]

It seems to me that my last argument against the life-technique of collage is also my strongest one. In the program "fest into everyday life," the realization of utopian freedom and festive existence is at stake—and not permanent compromising and idealized discontinuity between everyday life and that reality which is more than everyday life. There is at stake the realization of values which are counter to the vast majority of the established society, of a counterculture which aims at a radical change in culture and lifestyle. To argue with the German theorist of subculture, Rolf Schwendter, a new strategy is at stake, which should simultaneously and equally avoid adjustment, isolation, and stiffening. The objectives of the strategy run from the creation of a countermilieu to self-organization, from the creation of "liberated zones" to the disintegration of the system into sociopolitical counterorganizations, without ignoring the contradictions in the subcultural opposition and especially in its economics.

Thus in the struggle between the majority's values and countervalues there might come into existence a political program toward the "self-organization of one's needs" in the dialectic of integration and opposition, of *yes* and *no*. For under the given conditions of our society, only such a dialectic promises to be effective, since it leads neither into a final unpolitical isolation, though it might be verbally radical, nor into a too smooth adjustment. Counterculture and subculture do mean, in any case, "liberation of everyday life"; they are searching for "models of a communal life without the pressure of efficiency, frustration, and anxiety," to quote the title of another German contribution to the counterculture debate (8).

Although my book does not claim to be written out of or for the counterculture, I nevertheless regard this movement as the most realistic and utopian resort for the "creation of a world in which it will be easier to love" (Paulo Freire).

Fest and everyday life of the counterculture and of those who sympathize with it are different from the arrangements of the vast majority. The "collage" becomes dynamic and directed toward a specific goal. Fest as a transcended everyday life cannot be merely good for relaxation. Nor can it have the characteristics of a reducing valve and become nothing more than compensation. On the contrary, fest can become the standard of the common human everyday life in the future. That social-philosophical theory of a "metamorphosis of the everyday reality" toward fest which is theoretically most convincing may be Henri Lefebvre's critique of everyday life (39, 39). Since the time of the French resistance in the Second World War he has demanded a "break with the everyday, the restitution of fest" (39, 36) in view of the end of economic shortages and the end of conventional urban life. This should affect the revolutionary dissolution, transformation, and new organization of everyday reality and should bring to an end the differentiation between fest and everyday life, which has been misused politically.

These revolutionary aims, however, are frozen in a society which is perfectly bureaucratized and in which consumption is completely directed, although at its basis it is irrational. That

53

is why these revolutionary aims are neutralized bureaucratically and institutionally. Lefebvre's political publications are the French equivalent of Marcuse's *One-Dimensional Man.* The human being is manipulated, creatively impotent, an automaton of consumption; "by the indirect agency of everyday life," society is "cyberneticized," "structured," and "functionalized" (39, 64).

> If [dramatic] tragedy still exists it is out of sight; the "cool" prevails. Everything is ostensibly dedramatized; instead of tragedy there are objects, certainties, "values," roles, satisfactions, jobs, situations and functions. Yet there are powers, colossal and despicable, that swoop down on everyday life and pursue their prey in its evasions and departures, dreams and fantasies, to crush it in their relentless grip. [39, 65]

Nevertheless Lefebvre—even more so than Marcuse—believes in the power of old and new contradictions, which might be able to break off again the predesigned everyday life as a product of roles, programs, institutions, and merchandise. It is important that his program begins with the everyday life in which society has become entangled and has frozen itself. "Starting with the everyday reality," society should be overcome within itself (39, 203ff.). It is this starting point (everyday life) from which Lefebvre's revolutionary process views *"the Festival rediscovered* and magnified by overcoming the conflict between everyday life and festivity" (39, 206).

So countercultural liberation of everyday life can create the new atmosphere of festivity, whose structures stand out only against the horizon. That is why it is no wonder that even people who belong to the counterculture still make clear distinctions between fest and everyday life. But because their fests look different and must look different from those of the majority, a new debate about ritual and play has emerged in Germany, especially among a group called the "hedonistic left," which tries to continue the antiauthoritarian elements within the student movement.

Ritual and Play

For the early antiauthoritarian as well as for all liberal theories of fest and play, the term *ritual* and the actuality of ritual have a negative aftertaste or even main taste. In the negative sense ritual is thought of as a rigid, solemn ceremony. One associates it with form, uniform, and military parades, and at the extreme even with ritual murder. Because rituals can be repeated and actually are repeated, one associates with them the psychoanalytical term "coercion of repetition," with all of its negative connotation. "An intolerable feeling of guilt because of libidinous or aggressive impulses which belong to the basic drives" (55, 371) can lead to compulsively repeated private ceremonies, to secret ridiculous rituals, which block other activities, interactions with the world, and the ability to love. According to Freud there might really exist a resemblance between "neurotic ceremonials and the sacred acts of religious ritual" (21, 119). This can be seen first "in the qualms of conscience brought on by their neglect, in their complete isolation from all other actions . . . and in the conscientiousness with which they are carried out."

Rituals in general, neurotic coercions of repetition such as prayers and elements of liturgy, including distribution and acceptance of the sacrament, might assume "the value of defense and protection" (21, 123). They could be a conscious or unconscious confession of guilt and at the same time the attempt to master it on a more or less magical level. In a symbolic event the ritual participant performs what is forbidden, but at the same time punishes himself or herself in the fixation and in the coercive character of the event's procedure. According to Freud, "a progressive renunciation of constitutional instincts, whose activation might afford the ego primary pleasure, appears to be one of the foundations of the development of human civilization" (21, 127). And Freud thinks that this kind of renunciation or instinctual repression also promotes religion. If psychoanalysis indeed wants to make a contribution to the liberation of human beings from unconscious coercions and feelings of guilt, it has to bring to consciousness the conflicts which lie behind such coercions, rituals, and attempts at magic in the life of the individual as well as the given culture and religion, and it has to work through them. Although Freud has tried to derive all religion, including the Christian religion, albeit with some differentiation, out of the "sense of guilt and the remorse attaching to it" (22, 146), one should ask whether it is only a falsely contrived and falsely practiced Christianity which is a religion of guilt and guilt complexes. In the last chapter this question will be briefly discussed.

In the present context only this much can be made clear: Rituals, which carry with them the character of coercion and which are not utterly separated from magic, cannot be harmonized with our starting definition of fest. Coercion and magic are not proper means to enlarge and intensify consciousness and life. On the contrary, they prevent such increase and hinder primal affects and impulses. Freud from his perspective was ready to understand culture generally as a system of coercions and renunciations of drives. Such a culture may offer fests as "excess," in which usual prohibitions are broken in a ceremonial way (22, 140). This breakthrough, however, is connected with self-punishment; so it turns out to be an attempt of liberation *within* the given religion and culture and their systems of suppression, and as such it must fail. For according to therapeutical praxis, a "ritual which is correctly repeated in a totemistic way" will not "solve the problem of guilt" (56, 145).

Has the debate about ritual and fest come to an end before it has begun? Are there rituals which are not affiliated with magic and coercion?

There is a definition and a reality of rituals beyond pathology, beyond the fixation on the problem of guilt. Ritual attitude can be neutrally described as an interaction between two or more persons, which usually can be and will be repeated, and which is more than merely verbal. The fact that it can be repeated is based on the systems of rules behind the happening. According to this neutral understanding, ritual interactions and festive ceremonies can be a confirmation of consent, a "periodical reaffirmation" of shared religious, aesthetical, and moral definitions of values and norms of behavior (18, 604). It is clear that one should take into consideration such rituals in the theory and practice of fest, especially if the unneurotic person is also "born with the need for such regular and mutual affirmation and certification" (18, 604). Ritualization is a highly personal matter, and is yet group-bound; by the same token it heightens a sense both of *belongingness* and of personal *distinctiveness*. It is *playful*, and yet *formalized*, and this in details as well as in the *whole* procedure. Becoming *familiar* through repetition, it yet renews the *surprise* of recognition which provides a catharsis of affects. . . . Could it be, then, that true ritualization represents a creative *formalization* which avoids both impulsive excess *and* compulsive self-restriction, both social *anomie* and moralistic *coercion*? [18, pp. 605, 507–08]

It is evident that especially those groups who shape up their lives (for example, living in communes and using drugs) in opposition to the vast majority are in need of such ritualistic-symbolic reaffirmation.

They need such stabilization, since *their* common values and aims are not stable and not without problems. So they have to reassure their lifestyle. The stability of the majority consists in the fact that everyday life is precontrived and that unquestionable self-evident attitudes toward fest channel the life of body and soul. The year finds its order, norms, and rhythms by Sundays and festive days, and everyday finds it by labor, traffic, and mass media (cf. 39; also cf. 4). Civilization at large integrates most of the people, even if they are mentally or physically ill. The representatives of the various smaller subgroups are opposed precisely to this vast integration; in this opposition, however, they will lose themselves hopelessly as individuals if they do not succeed in setting up a counterintegration. That is why subcultures also need *their* own integrations, *their* norms, orders, and rhythms—and also *their* rituals, by means of which position and negation, agreement and opposition, *yes* and *no* are simultaneously reaffirmed.

Even if one agrees with such a positive understanding of ritual, it still makes sense to distinguish clearly between ceremonial rituals and more festive, celebrative play and game activities. At the same time, however, the interrelationship between ritual and play has to be defined. Otherwise, ritual's tendency toward coercion and its "integrative undertow" with the accompanying elements of formation, conformism, control, and its threat of sanctions (cf. 33, 25) can end up only postponing the real problems. In that case the danger would arise that the needs of human drives would be again merely diverted, and rituals would continue to support "a repressive and magically oriented" culture (33, 32). But whenever play *and* ritual stay together, play will not end up in individual playfulness, which leads to asocial isolated subjectivity.

The relationship between ritual and play has been recently discussed by Diethart Kerbs and Otto Seydel. For Kerbs, play represents impartiality and immediacy, Dionysian negation and suspension of all renunciations of human drives; play "belongs to a culture which is oriented toward emancipation and intellect" (33, 32). Rituals, on the other hand, are "essentially for the establishment of social organizations" (60, 508), because they produce "stable norms of attitude and schemes of thinking in the context of a group." So they effect "for each single person emotional security and relief of decisions, without which human beings can not exist"; they effect the "social feelings of being safe" and "cognitive consistency" (60, 510). But precisely in view of these effects, "playful attitudes can prevent the ritual as norm and order from absolutizing itself" (60, 513). Such a relationship leads to the twofold guiding principle, "Ritual may perhaps lead persons out of apathy, but not into freedom. Play is only anticipation of freedom—if one wills, also the exercise of freedom—but not the realization of liberation" (33, 33; cf. 60, 512).

Rites of Passage

The discussion about the distinction and relationship between ritual and play would be concluded too quickly if the meaning of these terms on their own were not dealt with further. In the history of religion and in anthropology the term *ritual* has an additional aspect, which has not been taken into consideration so far. Rituals have here also the function of stabilization. But this definition of its function is not sufficient. A great amount of anthropological material can prove that stabilizing rituals are used especially in crisis situations of a tribe or an individual, with the intention of accompanying persons from one stage of life to another, from one place of settlement to another, from existence to non-existence, and from non-existence to existence. Such rituals, as they can still be found today in the liturgies of baptism, confirmation, marriage, and funeral, are called rites of passage. They separate persons and communities ritually and sacramentally from what has become old, liberate them from bad spirits and alien powers, accompany them in the transition to a new existence, and finally incorporate them in the new reality. Ritually the old is addressed with *no* and the new with *yes*, and so the new *yes* rules over the old one. As an illustration, the Lord's Supper still has today the element of renunciation of sin, that is, of the old life, and the element of incorporation into the body of Christ as an incorporation into him: "This is my blood. . . ."

Thus rituals can intend not only the stabilization or possibly the restitution of an old situation, but they can also lead through excess, a restitution of the chaos which reigned in the beginning, to a *new* order, to really new conditions. They have functioned in this way throughout the history of human beings. Often enough it was not merely a matter of a *game* of *exchange* and confusion, as with the medieval Feast of Fools, for example, but a real and effective *change* and transformation. The participants in this fest began anew, and it was not merely a fresh start with the old situation. They began after everything that was available had been exchanged—roles, garments, names, wives, and properties (cf. 13). Such excessive breaks with the old life, saturnalian artificial gaps between before and after, naturally cannot be reintroduced at will any time. But in dealing with the present and the future of fest one may come to this conclusion: in correspondence to the tradition of rites of passage, festive rituals and games should not simply flow back into an unchanged everyday life; rather they should enable the emergence of new elements in everyday life. Only then would the festive person be empowered not to revert simply to being *homo faber*. And only this would be adequate to the messianic program, according to which fest should come into everyday life. This messianic program, however, would correspond to its Messiah; Jesus *before* Golgatha, the Jesus who passed *through* the chaos of the cross, death and hell, was different from the Easter Christ of faith.

Play and the "Cycle of Activation"

Not only the term *ritual* but also the term *play* has a meaning which has not been mentioned so far, but which is important in the context of fest and everyday life. Kerbs and Seydel have used the term *play* with different meanings. For Kerbs, ritual and play are similar to each other because he construes *both* as "a happening between persons, which follows certain rules, which can be repeated, and which is staged" (33, pp. 25, 29). For Seydel, however, play is defined as a radical "countermode to ritualistic behavior," and therefore it cannot be repeated and can hardly be limited by rules (60, 511). I will not deal with this distinction here. It seems to reflect the distinction between *game* and *play*, which cannot be made in the German language (in which the translation of both terms is *Spiel*). This distinction is important also because by it one can differentiate play and game activities in various stages of life. It seems more important in our context to ask whether there is a perspective on the reality of play and game which can be at all helpful in describing the reality of fest. In what sense can a festive person be *homo ludens*?

Here I would like to integrate an important contribution of Heinz Heckhausen, "Approach to a Psychology of Play." Among the characteristics of play cataloged by Heckhausen, the "cycle of activation" seems to be especially interesting for our purposes. With this term he means a search for a specific "alteration of tensions and solving of these tensions" within "an undifferentiated framework of aims and an immediate perspective of time" (25, 226–27). In play activities children and adults seek increasing tensions, but they also seek a joyful solving as soon as possible. But here they do not aim at a complete settlement of these tensions, not at a total psychic or physical balance. Rather, they immediately seek another graduation of tensions. A child who has been found in his or her hiding place is ready to continue and to begin hide-and-seek anew. On the other hand, if the tensions increase too much, the child will throw himself or herself upon the ground or even run to meet his or her pursuer. Heckhausen distinguishes different elements by means of which playful tensions can be set up: novelty, or the *change* from an old to a new experience, is exciting and causes tensions. Furthermore, games and play must have *surprising effects.* Then we find a discrepancy, not between old and new, but between now and later. Or the arrangement of the playground as such, that is, the conditions of time and space in which one has to act, can in itself be thrilling. Then the conditions and the rule systems are rather complex and will not be fully figured out at once. Entanglement and complexity create tensions. Finally, a "measure of *risk* and *danger*" belongs to the tensions games may produce (25, 231; cf. 230–31).

I would assume that 1) rhythms of tension/solving and new tensions, 2) surprising moments, 3) complexity, and 4) risk are useful elements for various modes of the dramatization of fest, since fest is an artificially and aesthetically constructed environment of time and space. In any case, I am convinced that in a theory of fest it makes sense to take over Heckhausen's term *cycle of activation.* Heckhausen on his own concedes that it might be useful to understand not only games but also other activities from this perspective. Then, however, we will discover different processes and intensities of tensions and different resolutions of them.

In any case, by taking the "cycle of activation" over into my theory of fest I underscore once more that celebration does not mean a continuing decreasing of tensions, a relaxation of mere dysfunctionality, or a negation of bad tensions. Rather, celebration begins with and finds its very essence in the creation of countertensions and different processes of tensions. Neither is fest defined by the quietness of Sunday as such or by the "relaxation of a holiday" (10, 214). Although in the context of his "anthropology of fest" Otto F. Bollnow later deals with increased joy of life and overflowing fullness (10, 232ff.), his initial description of the festive day can be misunderstood:

> One lives toward the festive day, one looks forward to it and marshals all one's energy to reach it and to complete the necessary work before it comes. But then on the festive day one comes to rest and quietude in order afterwards to come back with new vitality into the stream of time. [10, 212]

One should not, of course, underestimate the element of meditation, tranquility, and peaceful rest which belongs to Eden. But, on the other hand, is not fest also a kind of an exhaustion of energy, unrest, and activity on a level which is different from everyday? Does quietude really produce "new vitality" and energy? Is not rather the economy of forces activated and increased instead of being reduced toward balance and passivity?

Another reason to take the "cycle of activation" over into my theory of fest is that by it mere play activities can be more clearly discriminated from fests. For whereas "a time structure with the least possible organization and hierarchical form and a time perspective with short intervals constitute the amusement of play" (25, 237), a fest may also include such "cycles of activation" with short intervals and such amusement, but it is not sufficiently defined by that. Rather, such play activities are included in a much more complex tension-span and in a much more structured time perspective, which brings together meals, dances, artistic performances, and so on. Unlike a childlike experience of reality and a child's birthday party, everyday life as well as the fest of grown-ups has a "far anticipating time perspective" and a "complex time structure of basic activities and instrumental by-plays" (25, 241).

It seems to me that there appears here the limit of all sorts of regression which I recommended above. Children live too much in the given situation and in their immediate present to be able to comprehend larger contexts of different games and periods of fest. Festive expansion of consciousness and life cannot consist in a reduction of and regression from the full scale of one's experiential abilities, toward childlike limited measures. "Regression" here would have to mean integration of immediate and naive childlike relationships to the world into the world of the grown-ups. In that case, "unless you become like children" (Matt. 18:3) would not imply "ring around the roses." Rather, it would mean breaking through the limited adult consciousness which has become adjusted to reality. It would mean liberating the adult consciousness from the usual ways of control and direction through which one deprives oneself of the fullness of available reality, its impression and expression.

Fest and Ceremony

The differentiation between ritual and play can stimulate a final distinction in the framework of a theory of fest, that between fest and ceremony. Though the distinction might not be convincing and clear at all on the level of language, it might make sense in a phenomenological way. Ceremonies always make the impression of being more structured, and to that extent they are close to ritualistic attitudes. In ceremony (*Feier*), as Bollnow puts it, "all natural and free expressions of life" are suppressed by "consciously structured, stylized movements" (10, 227). Ceremony is a special event, a "ceremonious" act, characterized by a certain solemnity, by pathos, dark rooms, full colors, and serious music (10, 222ff.), whereas fest is lighter, less pathetical, brighter, more joyous. And in all that it is closer to play.

Ceremonies usually have historical or biographical reasons— marriage, examinations, the end of a war—which might occasionally overlap. Fest, on the other hand, can be the expression of the joy of life without a special external reason. Furthermore, ceremonies, similar to ritual encounters, intend to amalgamate even more a group which is already close, whereas fest carries with it more openness and consequently the possibility of distance, anonymity, staying at the edge, later coming and earlier leaving. Fests have no sociogram which can be fully designed ahead of time. That is why they are much more risky than ceremonies. A ceremony, whenever it is correctly prepared, is structured in such a way that it cannot be disturbed from within; it proceeds. But a fest can be successful or unsuccessful, however optimally it is prepared. The mood of solemnity can be produced liturgically; in any case, one can exclude countermoods. Joy and high spirits, however, cannot be produced. Fests can fail from misunderstandings, displeasure, or low spirits. The perfect ceremony is not familiar with misunderstandings and proceeds beyond the alternative of success or failure.

Once more the criterion "enlargement and intensification of life and consciousness" can help avoid reductions which take place too quickly and facilely. With a reasonable comprehension of history and psychology one cannot ignore the distinctions between fest and ceremony as they are made by Bollnow and especially Ernst Jünger. Successful community, increased joy of life, a "cheerfulness which is available to everybody" (29,

180), are and will remain something different from the seriousness of cult and liturgy whenever worldly festivity and dancing in the circle of finite life are different from the ceremonious experience of the limits, or even the loss of self and world which can accompany ecstasy. Both, however, fest and ceremony, belong to the fullness of the experience of reality. For us, ceremonies are more inaccessible than fests. But precisely they and their rituals belong to that kind of festivity whose psychological and social meaning, despite its possible misuse, is continuously but with great difficulty rediscovered.

It thus may be evident that there can be after all a clear distinction between ceremonies and fests in general. However, also here—just as with the elements of ritual and game—the relationship of that which is discriminated is more important than the mere discrimination as such. It seems to me that fest is a broader term which covers more different levels. Fest can contain ceremonial elements in itself. This is the case in Bachtin's view, in which the "world turned upside down" includes the official world. According to the model of Heckhausen, ceremony would be the maintained tension, a serious tightness which is solved only by the following fest and which is replaced by tension-spans which work on shorter periods and are more relaxed and joyful. Similarly, according to Bachtin, sacrament is replaced by excess and liturgy by the people's entertainment, although as far as time and space are concerned they are very close together. Thus the total event of *fest* as an all-inclusive term would consist of the alternation of more ceremonial and more festive elements.

But the ceremonial one would come first. The severe gravity would be the first step out of everyday life, fully liturgically shaped; and perhaps only this period of ceremonial tranquility would make possible the transformation of everyday life into a total fest. Otherwise, without this element of a rite of passage, without the change from one situation to a really different one, fest would too easily fall back into common unchanged everyday life.

5.

THESES TOWARD THE
REFORM OF WORSHIP

The theory of messianic fest presented so far implies some basic guidelines for worship and other festive activities in the Christian congregation. These guidelines will not be repeated here in detail, but the main point should be elaborated: there must remain a relation between fest and everyday world. Fest may not be just a means to tolerate and compensate for the everyday world or a means to neutralize bad vibrations. Fest should bring together elements of affirmation and protest as did Old Testament fests when they issued blessings as well as curses, benedictions as well as anathemas, confession of the true God as well as denial of the false ones. The general question for any kind of fest is that of whether it contributes to the increasing of awareness of self and world or whether it effects—more or less evidently—an impoverishment of affects, a dimming of consciousness, and additional restrictions and prohibitions in terms of experience and compulsive emotions. For there might be types of fest in which enlargement and intensification of consciousness and life are hiddenly or even openly hindered and forbidden.

This project of setting forth a theory of fest would become unbalanced if the final chapter were to enter into an extensive and intensive discussion of the ongoing theoretical and practical debate on the reform and renewal of worship. If in the whole conceptual approach developed here the relation between fest and everyday life is at stake, the renewal of worship can be merely *one* aspect of the renewal of Christian life. The following theses are not by any means a defense of the importance or the final aim of my approach. Nevertheless, I think it quite proper that a theory of messianic fest try to contribute to the debate on worship and other festive activities in the church. For all particular reforms of *worship* which do not reach the horizon of a broader theory and praxis of *fest*, however enthusiastic they might be, fall inevitably into the danger of remaining shortsighted and superficial.

The theses of this chapter form a unit on their own. With references to what has gone before, and also with short repetitions of formulae and interpretations, they seek to construct as coherent an argument as possible. The first two theses are intended to continue the more general debate of the preceding chapters in relation to the subject of this chapter: can the church be regarded as a counterculture? Is the Christian religion a religion of guilt?

Thesis 1: *Messianic churches and messianic groups in the churches are progressive subcultures or countercultures.*

As a matter of fact, churches are institutions with economic, social, educational, and religious activities. The church is *one* agency of socialization in society, especially for those who are not fully integrated in society, namely, children, adolescents, and senior citizens. In any case, the influence of the churches is related to the total social reality, although they are somewhat more private organizations in the United States than they are in most parts of Europe. If churches do not have a messianic orientation they will produce reactionary and merely affirmative results. They will stabilize and affirm the actual or given society in a religious way. The mainline church then is an agency of "civil religion," as Rousseau described it, and will affirm the common belief in "the existence of an almighty God, a wise Providence, the life to come, the reward of virtue and the punishment of vice" (49, 28). Such a civil religion can be criticized in accordance with Freud's plea for the increasing of the "principle of reality" as he has developed it in his book *The Future of an Illusion*. But then every church group which in this sense is not an agency of civil religion would have to be described sociologically in a neutral way as "subculture" or "counterculture." Countercultures are defined by their countervalues over against the majority of the established society. These countervalues in terms of education, social engagement, organization of leisure time, and interpretation of reality can be either conservative-regressive or messianic-progressive.

Churches will be *regressive* whenever they, in correspondence to the social separation of art and life, totally separate religion and society. The consequence of such a separation will be—corresponding to a cheap and merely aesthetic compensatory reconciliation in society—a religious and ritualistic reconciliation. Such a reconciliation in worship is like a religious narcotic consolation and is realized in a reduced life-scale. "Regressive" in this context means going back behind the actual problems and frontiers of oneself and society and avoiding conflict. It should not be misconstrued with its more positive connotation in other parts of this book, where it means taking one step back in order to make a step forward to integration of different areas of life and experience. Any kind of narcotization and reduction, however, contradicts the messianic understanding of festivity and celebration as well as every kind of enlargement and intensification of consciousness and life. As an agency of superstition, regressive religion reaffirms and produces anxieties, fixations, and illustrations and encourages magical and quasi-magical activities.

Churches become *progressive* countercultures whenever they realize "anticipations and alternatives toward a more humane future" (48, 13). Insofar as they remain within the messianic perspective, they will run into stiff opposition from the majority. They will form "liberated zones," even sociopolitical counterorganizations. (In the past we find such counterorganizations with a different lifestyle, for example, in monasticism and left-wing Reformation movements.) Such churches will create a countermilieu and will organize the requirements of their common life on their own. In doing so they should nevertheless keep contact with the majority, so that they will not abandon their possible influence by means of personal and institutionalized interactions with the majority.

If messianic churches can actually be understood as progressive countercultures, then the discussion about fest in the secular counterculture must be taken into consideration in theory and practice of the church, too. Ceremonies and celebrations can then be affirmations and realizations of their life, their values, and their aims. And if the big church organizations are pluralistic associations of different groups (some of which tend to be embodiments of civil religion, while others might be progressive as well as regressive countercultures), then, in any case, we must be able to envision and practice totally different types of worship and celebration.

Thesis 2: *Messianic belief is not a religion of guilt, but its overcoming.*

According to Freud, we can understand all kinds of religion as derived from awareness of guilt and repentance (22). This means that doctrines and rituals, liturgies and prayers, try to solve the problem of guilt in a magical way. If we must understand the Christian religion within this framework, then Christianity would be mere collective, coerced neurosis and would become fixated in a repetition of coercions. The result would be that the intensification of consciousness and life and the liberating rites of passage, as well as the games and celebrations which are derived from these experiences, would be impossible. But according to the testimonies of the New Testament, messianic belief is the end, the eschatological breaking off of moralistic and ceremonial law. The kingdom of God is a qualitatively new eschatological situation which encompasses the understanding and the reality of God, of human beings, and of the world.

The baptism which was practiced by John was already an eschatological sacrament. Enacted once for all, it prepared people for the ultimate judgment, precisely in contradiction to the other baptism movements of those days. Jesus keeps this eschatological dimension. But whereas John announces the judge of the world, Jesus first of all announces the coming of the kingdom of God and repentance in accordance with this.

So John preaches the *law* of repentance: the judge is near. Jesus preaches the *joy* of repentance: the reality of peace, justice, and freedom is near.

Repentance in the message of Jesus is misunderstood when it is construed as the act of confessing sins, contrition, ritualistic forgiveness—and then once again the cycle of sin, confession and so forth. In the message of Jesus the call of repentance was *one* element, beside and together with his reinterpretation of the Old Testament Law and his message of the kingdom of God. Here the reality of the kingdom of God seems to be the pivotal point, in relation to which the other elements of his message can be understood. There is no way to start with Jesus as the preacher of repentance and as the bringer of the new law and to move from there to an adequate understanding of the nearness of the kingdom of God. If we start with his reinterpretation of the law, the kingdom of God will be nothing but the powerless symbol of his utopian ethics.

According to Jesus' parables and his own lifestyle, however, the kingdom of God enables human beings to live a new life *beyond* the law of fasting and rituals of purification, not *against* the law of love, whenever love is the central issue of the law. The kingdom of God has eschatological reality, and Jesus' miracles are foreshadowings of this reality. They happen in tune with the power of this kingdom. Over against the interpretation of the kingdom of God as an ethical postulate, as Kant and many representatives of the liberal theology in the last century put it, we must understand it as an ethical *and* aesthetical *and* religious reality to come. According to Jesus' life and teaching, human beings live already to some extent in the power of this kingdom. In this context, repentance means practice of life and thinking toward this new reality and toward the reality of love which will be fully realized in the kingdom of God. His reinterpretation of the law (of love) and his suspension of the law (as far as fasting and rituals of cleansing are concerned) are legitimized by this reality. The exemption from the coercion of the law gives persons the chance for new spontaneity and offers them a new scope of fantasy and love.

Further developments within the New Testament also point

in this direction. According to Paul, *euangelion* does not mean repeated forgiveness of individual sin or the incessant cycle of sin, regret, and pardon, but the liberation from the *power* of sin. *Euangelion* is more and another thing than reactivation of the strength to fulfill God's tasks. Again, it is more and another thing than continuing correction of human insufficiency by means of merciful forgiveness. "If we live by the Spirit" (this is the overwhelming reality and presupposition!) "let us walk by the Spirit" (Gal. 5:25).

Overcoming of ritual religion is also one of the main issues of the letter to the Hebrews, although this letter holds completely to the images of the Old Testament and tries to explain the new reality with these old images. According to this letter, Jesus Christ is priest and sacrifice in one person; the high priest, the sacrificer, sacrifices himself away. Since he is sacrifice and sacrificer in one person, his actions mean that there is no longer a sacrificer or a high priest. So he brings the Old Testament religion of cult and sacrifice to its end (although the image of the priest remains with different functions: Jesus is now the *heavenly* priest).

In Christianity the ritualistic, magical, and coercive attempt to deal with the problem of sin and guilt essentially has been overcome. Guilt, however, remains both as an issue for Christian ethics (problems of punishment, resocialization, and so on) and as an expression for the gap between the holy God and the not-yet-reconciled world, a gap which can not be treated magically. What are the consequences of this for celebration and worship?

First of all the Lord's Supper cannot be understood, in Freud's terms, as a repeated elimination of the *father*, as a repetition of the deed, which demands atonement (22, 140–46; cf. 56, 177). Nor can it be understood as a constant repetition of the sacrifice of the son's life. According to Paul, the Lord's Supper is the participation in and distribution of the power of atonement in the death of Christ, which is ratified by God. Here again, confusion of symbol systems is always possible and has happened throughout the church's history. But such confusion might be avoided if we would understand the Lord's Supper in our churches as the celebration of an event which has been settled and completed, which really needs nothing more except our awareness of it. So the Lord's Supper is the celebration of the presence of Christ, who has died once for all; it is the proclamation of the presence of the God who reconciles.

If in the Christ event the universal religious game of coercion and repetition of guilt and atonement has been settled and completed, messianic faith cannot be fixed on the inhibition of guilt. Rather, it must be understood as a religion of the Son and of the brothers and sisters, and its theology cannot be a history of neurotic guilt, but a history of salvation and liberation.

It may be concluded that breaking off the coercion of repetition does not exclude, but includes a festive and joyful *renewal* of life, which is no longer ritual and magical. Although messianic life should be new as a whole, it is realized within the old world and against the resistance of the old world. So there remains the need for renewal, reassurance and reaffirmation of the new understanding of God and human beings, and the reaffirmation of the intention to live and to think toward the messianic reality to come. *This* seems to be the very purpose of worship and celebration. If these renewals do not lose their connection with everyday life, they will be liturgies of liberation and of setting out on a new way. They will have nothing in common with rituals of coercion. Whenever such liturgies of renewal are not attempted and are no longer realized, we will find unmessianic resignation. And whenever the need for renewal is realized merely externally, we will find an absurd transference: new pews, new liturgies, new facades, new cars, new clothes, and dry cleaning of everything which resists strong chemical treatment. In these cases renewal is available as merchandise and is the antithesis of messianic renewal.

A final comment about gospel and liberation is appropriate here. I am quite convinced that there will not be any reasonable theology of political liberation if we do not start with a theology of religious liberation. That is why I lay stress upon liturgical renewal. The Christian faith may be effective in terms of political and technological kinds of alienation. But,

71

first of all, Christian faith liberates us from religious alienation: superstition, inhibition of guilt, fixations toward authorities, narrow ideologies, and religious infantilism, however profane or sacred they might be.

Thesis 3: *Messianic theory and practice of fest appropriates and begins with traditions coming from the Bible and church history. That is why messianic fests do not happen in the present without a horizon, nor do they merely celebrate this present in itself. Rather, they are acted out in relation to memory and expectation.*

Whenever people are not totally assimilated to the ongoing everyday situation, their impressions will not come exclusively from present institutions and the mass media, and their experiences will not be limited to institutions and mass media. People can have different *im*pressions at the same time through the *ex*pressions and the lives of different and former people. Enlargement and intensification of consciousness and life always also means increasing historical awareness. If one only listens within oneself, one will get answers in terms of feeling and experience solely out of oneself and out of one's biographical and social context—and this may be too little. The Christian believer, however, will relate his or her own experiences and expectations in life and thought with the expectations and experiences which the Christian witnesses reflect. Precisely with these witnesses he or she experiences the difference between present facts and the past, and between present desires and the future. Such an experience of difference might be painful, but at the same time it creates a contradiction to one's present and opens up hope. So the messianic church is a community of memories and hopes; its fests activate memory and mobilize hope.

Remembrance of the past may give rise to dangerous insights, and the established society seems to be apprehensive of the subversive contents of memory. Remembrance is a mode of dissociation from the given facts, a mode of "meditation" which breaks, for short moments, the omnipresent power of the given facts. Memory recalls the terror and the hope that passed. [41, 98]

Today fewer and fewer people live their lives in the temporal dimension of history. That is why men are more and more absorbed in semiconscious states. For our five senses and all units of time which are shorter than a year will not have an awakening effect on our consciousness at all. [53, 49]

Thesis 4: *Liturgical expression will never be an adequate expression of that by which people are impressed and which forces them to expression. So expression in any case will be "only" a symbolical one. The symbolic character of symbols must be kept in mind, otherwise misunderstood symbols will lead to taboos and fixations. One might succeed in this by means of a playful treatment of symbols (just as some medieval excesses did).*

My basic claim is that increased consciousness must be expressed in life. The experience of the love of God reveals itself in my ability to love, and in everyday life it is conceivable for me and others only in this way. Messianic faith is not to be found merely in papers. Such faith, however, may also be expressed in *non*everyday life in liturgies, stories, and fests. These expressions must keep their *symbolic* character. This means that they mediate messianic reality, but at the same time refer to something beyond themselves. Otherwise liturgy might be confounded with life. Liturgy would become a substitute for life and would be mistaken for life. If this happens, liturgy will be misunderstood as magical mediation, as a magical agency of love. Magic, however, is an inappropriate attempt to enlarge and intensify experience and life. Symbols, on the other hand, represent such enlargement precisely within a certain space and in a certain time.

Liturgical and symbolical interactions can be misunderstood ceremonially and can lead to numbness because of the fact that they happen in places and times which are set aside exclusively for them. Such wrong fixations will be eliminated if the behavior in such spaces and times occasionally undergoes a paradigmatic change. Students who have effected a functional change in a normal order of worship (that is, discussion instead of liturgy and sermon, and so on) no longer experience this space as filled with taboos, as a peculiar space in which spontaneous, free, and different sorts of communication are not allowed. This is exactly the reason why they continue to attend the services.

In the medieval Feast of Fools and Feast of Asses I observe this kind of dismantling of the magical and ceremonial misunderstandings. The fascination of these feasts is not the exhibitionism or the obscenities which might have been involved. More than that and over against that, these excesses, as far as I can understand them, broke off false piety and ritual anxieties. As such they have had consequences for the total understanding of sacraments and liturgy. Indeed they can be viewed as already a liberated understanding of worship. The result would be, that cult, sacrament, and liturgy lose nothing except their affinity to taboo and magic. They would maintain and confirm their affinity to the reality of symbols. And so there is nothing wrong with the fact that the holy mass and the Lord's Supper can be celebrated after excess and parody. In fact it is just then that they become quite possible again, because they will be celebrated without the illusion of encountering the ultimate reality immediately within them or of handling this reality in terms of magic. "In a playful treatment of the symbols we experience their *provisional and human character*, and new ways of expression can be discovered" (60, 515).

Certainly we cannot reproduce medieval excesses today. But merely stable liturgical orders and ceremonies which are simply taken for granted can gain a new relativity by parody and play. Where they are not self-evident to some extent at least (which is true of nearly every element within the present worship activities in the liberal churches in Germany, for example), parody will mean making impossible any further liturgical use of these elements at all.

The problem of how to relate impressions and expressions— another issue of this thesis—is very severe in forms of mystical submersion and holy isolation. When the experiences of time

MAP
OF
FEST

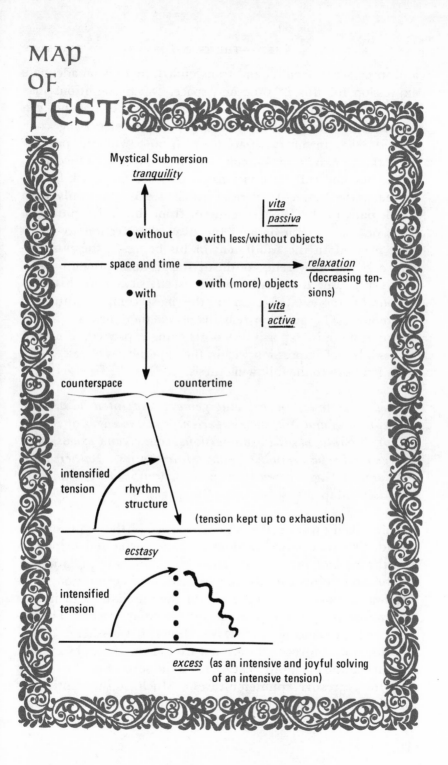

Mystical Submersion
tranquility

$\left|\dfrac{vita}{passiva}\right.$

● without   ● with less/without objects

space and time ⟶ *relaxation* (decreasing tensions)

● with   ● with (more) objects

$\left|\dfrac{vita}{activa}\right.$

counterspace   countertime

intensified tension   rhythm structure   (tension kept up to exhaustion)

ecstasy

intensified tension

excess (as an intensive and joyful solving of an intensive tension) and space are broken off and transcended, there is no adequate expression for this *in* time and space. Such conditions may occur in meditations and certain liturgical events, but they can be realized only in the individuals of the celebrating community. For in our civilization up to now (with the possible exceptions of some phenomena in the Pentecostal movement) we do not find collective visions, as they are practiced, for example, in the Native American Church (see 5). Certainly, even theologians in the Western church, from the early church fathers on, have claimed that "the utmost perfection to which man may attain the fulfillment of his being, is the *visio beatifica*," "seeing awareness of the divine ground of the universe" (51, 11ff). But the totality which is envisioned in this *visio* cannot be represented even in the most complex liturgical ceremony. The question remains of whether such a *visio beatifica*, if there is no possibility of its being expressed, should be a possibility of impression within the experiences of fest. This question leads to the following thesis.

Thesis 5: *If fest provokes enlargement and intensification of consciousness and life, then experiences at the edges of reality, as, for example, mystical submersions, ecstasy, and excess, must not generally be excluded in church festivities. Rather, these elements belong to ceremonies and celebrations throughout history* (see "Map of Fest" on preceding page).

Intensified joy as well as the experience of the limits of self, world, time, and space are human phenomena and belong to the theory and practice of fest. Messianic interpretation of celebration points to only one limitation of celebration: celebrations are not in accordance with the messianic idea if they realize less human love than in the everyday world. The example of the dancing King David shows that aesthetic, moral, and religious provocations are not excluded. This observation is in itself already a provocation for some sorts of civil religions and for regressive countercultures. Much of the continuing innocence and ineffectiveness of the recent liturgical reform movement is due not so much to the Pauline exhortation to treat carefully the weak members of the congregation, but rather to the fact that the reformers are themselves weak and anxiously avoid genuinely enlarged impressions and expressions, experiences of limits and borders of so-called reality.

An initial indication of these experiences would contain the following elements. *Mystical submersion* is the ultimate level of tranquility within fest. It is a totally different experience of time, or even a rupture through time, instead of a framework of countertime. Mystical submersion is the most radical alternative to any kind of production and consumption of the product, the ultimate experience of *vita passiva*.

Ecstasy and *excess*, on the other hand, can be understood as the ultimate experiences of *vita activa*. Excess is the expression of an extremely intensive solving of a tension which has had equal intensity, whereas ecstasy is the expression and self-realization of an utmost intensified and maintained tension. Such ecstasy as ultimate presence and highest tension *in* time and space is the opposite to tranquility, on the one hand, and to relaxation, on the other. From the economic point of view, it is radical attrition of power. In a visionary abundance of images as well as in dancing, tensions will not be solved as they are in excess with extreme joy, but they are intensified more and more in a cycle of activations up to complete exhaustion. In contrast to conditions of meditation and mystical submersions, such ecstatic conditions are creations in and of time and space with very sophisticated and complex structures and rhythms. As such, they break through concrete and everyday experience of time and space. Finally, ecstasy as utmost intensified and maintained tension, together with its solution, before the radical exhaustion happens, can be understood as the absolute limit of every possible cycle of activation.

Thesis 6: *The variety of different possibilities of expression and impression within the framework of fest should find its concrete realization in complex structures of different units within the context of large fests.*

This is why I cannot plead for a playful distortion of *all* liturgical elements within worship activities or for a changing and negation of such activities in favor of completely unliturgical celebrations in Christian congregations consisting of nothing but games, dispersal of information, and activities of socialization. This would mean a loss of reality and concrete possibilities. On the one hand, I agree that it is an absurd situation when a Christian congregation is ready to participate only in the liturgy and is neither willing nor able to support and set up any other form of social and aesthetic communication. My aim is not at all the negation or substitution of worship activities, but rather the overcoming of the isolation of worship and the integration of worship activities into a larger context of celebration and life.

It will be here that the "metamorphosis of the everyday world" and the "restitution of celebration," in the sense of the French philosopher Henri Lefebvre, will happen. The restitution of celebration is possible as a radical transmutation and reorganization of everyday life within urban societies (39, pp. 39, 36).

BIBLIOGRAPHY

1. Alewyn, Richard. "Das grosse Welttheater." *Das grosse Welttheater. Die Epoche der höfischen Feste in Dokument und Deutung.* Edited by Richard Alewyn and K. Sälzle. rde, no. 92.

2. Bachtin, Michail. *Literatur und Karneval: Zur Romantheorie und Lachkultur.* Munich, 1969.

3. Barth, Karl. *Church Dogmatics.* Vol. 3. Edinburgh, 1936.

4. Benedict, Hans-Jürgen. "Der genormte Alltag. Die Ritualisierung des Lebens durch die Massenmedien." *Evangelische Kommentare* 5(1972):342–45.

5. Benz, Ernst. "Der Peyote-Kult in der Native American Church." *Religion und die Droge: Ein Symposion über religiöse Erfahrungen unter Einfluss von Halluzinogenen.* Edited by M. Josuttis and H. Leuner. Stuttgart, 1972. Pp. 23–37.

6. Berger, Peter L. *A Rumor of Angels: Modern Society and the Rediscovery of the Supernatural.* Garden City, N.Y., 1969.

7. Bernsdorf, Wilhelm. "Ventilsitten." *Wörterbuch der Soziologie.* Edited by W. Bernsdorf. 2d ed. Stuttgart, 1969. Pp. 1220–21.

8. Böckelmann, Frank. *Befreiung des Alltags. Modelle eines Zusammenlebens ohne Leistungsdruck, Frustration und Angst.* Munich, 1970.

9. Böhmer, H. "Narrenfest." *Realencyklopädie für protestantische Theologie und Kirche.* Vol. 13. 3d ed., 1903. Pp. 650ff.

10. Bollnow, Otto Friedrich. *Neue Geborgenheit: Das Problem einer Überwindung des Existentialismus.* 3d ed. Stuttgart, 1972.

11. Cardenal, Ernesto. *Das Buch von der Liebe.* Wuppertal, 1971.

12. Cox, Harvey. *The Feast of Fools: A Theological Essay on Festivity and Fantasy.* Cambridge, Mass., 1969.

13. Crawley, Ernest. *The Mystic Rose: A Study of Primitive Marriage.* London, 1902.

14. Feige, J., et al. *Dienste der Kirche in der Freizeitgesellschaft: Theses*. Gladbeck, 1972.

15. Drewes, G. M. "Zur Geschichte der fête des fous." *Stimmen aus Maria Laach* 47(1894):571–87.

16. Erikson, Erik H. *Identity and the Life Cycle*. New York, 1959.

17. ———. *Young Man Luther: A Study in Psychoanalysis and History*. New York, 1958.

18. ———. "Ontogeny of Ritualization." *Psychoanalysis—A General Psychology: Essays in Honor of Heinz Hartman*. Edited by R. M. Loewenstein et al. New York, 1966. Pp. 601–21.

19. "Fest im M.V. ein Gesellschaftsspiel." Vol. 1. Spielumwelt in der Neuen Gesellschaft für Bildende Kunst and the West Berlin Volkstheaterkooperative. N.D.

20. Flögel, Carl Friedrich. *Geschichte des Groteskekomischen: Ein Beitrag zur Geschichte der Menschheit*. Liegnitz und Leipzig, 1788.

21. Freud, Sigmund. "Obsessive Actions and Religious Practices." *The Standard Edition of the Complete Psychological Works of Sigmund Freud*. Translated by James Strachey. Vol. 9. London, 1959. Pp. 117–27.

22. ———. *Totem and Taboo: Resemblances Between the Psychic Lives of Savages and Neurotics*. New York, 1946.

23. Fromm, Erich. "Der Sabbath." *Psychoanalytische Interpretationen biblischer Texte*. Edited by Y. Spiegel. Munich, 1972. Pp. 174–84.

24. Gadamer, Hans-Georg. *Wahrheit und Methode: Grundzüge einer philosophischen Hermeneutik*. 2d ed. Tübingen, 1965.

25. Heckhausen, Heinz. "Entwurf einer Psychologie des Spielens," *Psychologische Forschung* 27(1963–64):225–43.

26. Hein, G. W. Arendsen. "Selbsterfahrung und Stellungnahme eines Psychotherapeuten." *Religion und die Droge: Ein Symposion über religiöse Erfahrungen unter Einfluss von Halluzinogenen*. Edited by M. Josuttis and H. Leuner. Stuttgart, 1972. Pp. 96–108.

27. Heinrich, Klaus. *Versuch über die Schwierigkeit nein zu sagen*. Frankfurt, 1964.

28. Huxley, Aldous. *The Doors of Perception: Heaven and Hell*. New York, 1963.

29. Jünger, Ernst. *Annäherungen: Drogen und Rausch*. Stuttgart, 1970.

30. Jungmann, Josef Andreas. "Das kirchliche Fest nach Idee und Grenze." *Verkündigung und Glaube: Festgabe für Franz X. Arnold.* Edited by T. Filthaut and J. A. Jungmann. Freiburg, 1958. Pp. 164–84.

31. Keen, Sam. *Apology for Wonder.* New York, 1969.

32. Kerbs, Diethart. Ästhetische Existenz und ästhetische Erziehung." *Beiträge zu einer Interaktions- und Theaterpädagogik: Aus Referaten und Diskussionen anlässlich der Musischen Wochen 1970.* Edited by Pädagogisches Zentrum. Berlin, 1970. Pp. 43–47.

33. ———. "Das Ritual und das Spiel: Bemerkungen über die politische Relevanz des Ästhetischen." *Die hedonistische Linke: Beiträge zur Subkultur-Debatte.* Edited by Diethart Kerbs. Neuwied and Berlin, 1970. Pp. 24–47.

34. Kolakowski, Leszek. *Geist und Ungeist christlicher Traditionen.* Stuttgart, 1971.

35. Kuhn, Helmut. *Das Sein und das Gute.* Munich, 1962.

36. Laing, Ronald D. *The Politics of Experience and the Bird of Paradise.* Baltimore, 1967.

37. Lange, Ernst. "Erwachsenenbildung in der Freizeitgesellschaft." *Das missionarische Wort* 23(1970):118–34.

38. Lec, Stanislaw Jerzy. *Neue unfrisierte Gedanken.* Munich, 1964.

39. Lefebvre, Henri. *Everyday Life in the Modern World.* Translated by Sacha Rabinovitch. London, 1971.

40. Lieberg, Godo. "Die Bedeutung des Festes bei Horaz." *Synusia: Festgabe für W. Schadewaldt.* Edited by H. Flashar and K. Gaiser. Pfullingen, 1965. Pp. 403–27.

41. Marcuse, Herbert. *One-Dimensional Man: Studies in the Ideology of Advanced Industrial Society.* Boston, 1968.

42. ———. *Das Ende der Utopie.* Berlin, 1967.

43. ———. *Eros and Civilization: A Philosophical Inquiry into Freud.* New York, 1962.

44. Martin, Gerhard Marcel. *"Wir wollen hier auf Erden schon . . ." Das Recht auf Glück.* Stuttgart, 1970.

45. ———. "Eine neue Genitiv-Theologie? Gibt es so etwas wie eine Theologie des Spiels." *Wissenschaft und Praxis in Kirche und Gesellschaft* 60(1971):516–23.

46. ———. "Der glückliche Christ: Theologische Reflexionen zum Thema Glück." *Das Glück der Tüchtigen/Das Glück der Süchtigen.* Wuppertal, 1972. Pp. 64–84.

47. Miller, David L. *Gods and Games: Towards a Theology of Play.* New York, 1970.

48. Moltmann, Jürgen. *Theology of Play.* Translated by Reinhard Ulrich. New York, 1972.

49. ———, et al. *Religion and Political Society.* New York, 1974.

50. Pannenberg, Wolfhart. *Was ist der Mensch?* 3d ed. Göttingen, 1968. Published in English as *What is Man?* Translated by Duane A. Priebe. Philadelphia, 1970.

51. Pieper, Josef. *In Tune with the World: A Theory of Festivity.* Translated by Richard and Clara Winston. New York, 1965.

52. Riesman, David. *The Lonely Crowd: A Study of the Changing American Character.* Garden City, New York, 1953.

53. Rosenstock-Huessy, Eugen. *Soziologie: Zweiter Band. Die Vollzahl der Zeiten.* Stuttgart, 1958.

54. Roszak, Theodore. *The Making of a Counter Culture: Reflections on the Technocratic Society and Its Youthful Opposition.* Garden City, N.Y., 1969.

55. Scharfenberg, Joachim. "Zum Religionsbegriff Sigmund Freuds." *Evangelische Theologie* 30(1970):367–78.

56. ———. *Sigmund Freud und seine Religionskritik als Herausforderung für den christlichen Glauben.* Göttingen, 1968.

57. Schmidt, C. "Eselsfest" *Realencyklopädie für protestantische Theologie und Kirche.* Vol. 5. 3d ed., 1898. Pp. 497–98.

58. Schutz, Roger. *Ein Fest ohne Ende.* Gütersloh, 1972.

59. Schwendter, Rolf. *Theorie der Subkultur.* Cologne and Berlin, 1971.

60. Seydel, Otto. "Spiel und Ritual. Überlegungen zur Reform des Gottesdienstes." *Wissenschaft und Praxis in Kirche und Gesellschaft* 60(1971):507–15.

61. Tillich, Paul. *The Courage to Be.* New Haven, 1952.

62. Vostell, Wolf. *Aktionen: Happenings und Demonstrationen seit 1965. Eine Dokumentation.* Hamburg, 1970.

63. Weidkuhn, Peter. "Fastnacht-Revolte-Revolution." *Zeitschrift für Religions- und Geistesgeschichte* 21(1969):289–306.